How to Survive in the Ministry

William L. Malcomson, editor

Judson Press ® Valley Forge

HOW TO SURVIVE IN THE MINISTRY

Library of Congress Cataloging in Publication Data
Main entry under title:

How to survive in the ministry.

Includes bibliographies.
Contents: Creating wholeness for the minister of tomorrow / John R. Landgraf—Self-directed education / William L. Malcomson—This matter of money / Terry L. Burch—Ad-ministering in the eighties / Leroy H. Sandberg—[etc.]
1. Pastoral theology—Addresses, essays, lectures.
I. Malcomson, William L.
BV4017.H68 253'.2 82-224
ISBN 0-8170-0964-7 AACR2

Printed in the U.S.A.

Contents

Contributors

Terry L. Burch has been a pastor. For the last seventeen years he has worked with the Ministers and Missionaries Benefit Board, the pension board of American Baptist Churches. In this capacity he has counseled with many pastors about their family finances.

Robert L. Charpentier is associate director of Career Counseling at the Center. As a Roman Catholic priest he has served in the pastorate and in counseling ministries for several years. He is a Diplomate of the American Association of Pastoral Counselors and a licensed Marriage, Family, and Child therapist.

Florence Fairhill is an ordained American Baptist minister who is the administrative assistant at the Center. Her other work experience has been in home missions and Christian education.

John R. Landgraf is director of Career Counseling at the Center. He has served as an evangelist, youth pastor, hospital chaplain, and pastoral counselor. An American Baptist, John is a Diplomate of the American Association of Pastoral Counselors.

William L. Malcomson is western director of Continuing and Theological Education Services for the Board of Educational Ministries of the American Baptist Churches. He has been a pastor, college professor, and a seminary professor and administrator.

Leroy H. Sandberg has been a pastor, a judicatory executive, and is, at present, the western personnel consultant for American Baptist Personnel Services. He has conducted workshops and taught ministerial management for professional church leaders and seminarians.

Introduction

This book is designed to help ministers and their spouses cope with living and ministering in the 1980s and 1990s. It is a difficult and challenging time to be alive, but a time which is, we believe, full of promise.

The following analyses and suggestions have grown out of the experiences of six ministers who are colleagues together in the Center for the Ministry in Oakland, California.[1] The Center for the Ministry emerged over a decade ago to address pressing concerns of ministers: better salaries, career development counseling, continuing education, and placement. Several agencies of the American Baptist Churches have cooperated to put the Center together, representatives of Educational Ministries, Personnel Services, and the Ministers and Missionaries Benefit Board. This "full-service bank" seeks to assist professional church leaders in their self-understanding and to help them put professional and personal resources to work effectively within the context of their functions as leaders within the church. We are engaged daily in career development counseling, as well as educational, financial, and personnel counseling and

[1] The Center for the Ministry, 7804 Capwell Drive, Oakland, CA 94621.

consulting. We teach, manage, preach, and lead groups of ministers, ministers' spouses, and laypersons. Our work is in the western states, primarily among American Baptists, but increasingly among many communions, Protestant and Roman Catholic.

As I read through the chapters in this book, two words which embody its key concepts stood out in my mind. The words are "intentionality" and "celebration." We feel that to cope successfully in the eighties and nineties involves a conscious, personal intention to change and grow, whether in self-care (chapter 1), learning (chapter 2), financial planning (chapter 3), managing (chapter 4), spiritual growth (chapter 5), or marriage (chapter 6). If we are passive, waiting for others to define who we are and what we should do, we will not make it through the latter part of the twentieth century with zest and competence. As your colleagues in ministry, we at the Center are convinced that we all must become more intentional, self-directing, and active. We believe that God is willing us to be this way.

We also celebrate. What do we celebrate? The recovering of wholeness (chapter 1), the new day in education (chapter 2), the excitement of administering (chapter 4), the possibilities of growing spiritually (chapter 5), the opportunities for creative spousehood (chapter 6), the advent of growing numbers of women in ministry (chapter 7), new ways of coping with success and failure (chapter 8), and the often overlooked but nonetheless significant work of the "silent ministers" (chapter 9).

God is at work in our time, creating wholeness, overcoming "dis-ease," and enabling persons to realize their gifts in more intentional and fulfilling ways. We celebrate God's work and our opportunities for participation in the ongoing creating of ministry.

William L. Malcomson

Creating Wholeness for the Minister of Tomorrow

John R. Landgraf

Chapter 1

Joe W. is a minister. He was reared within the mainstream of the Christian faith, and it seemed natural to him to hear and answer the "call." He finished college and seminary and has now been employed as a full-time pastor for twenty years in four different churches. At age forty-five he looks tired and is obviously overweight. When his defenses drop, he speaks of "burnout," a term he picked up somewhere which he knows has something to do with stress, overload, or battle fatigue. He made an appointment at the Center for the Ministry for career guidance, stating a desire to leave the ministry and retool for some other occupation.

Joe is, of course, apocryphal, a fictitious creation of my imagination. But he is also real. He is real because he typifies one kind of client we see at the Center for the Ministry—the minister who has "had it" with the ministry.

No one ever said the ministry would be easy. The apostle Paul characterized it as a battle. But battle or not, many ministers have viewed their lot as a happy and prosperous one—not in financial terms, but in the richness of friends and the satisfactions of work well done. They have exulted in the joy of making a difference in people's lives and have testified that they wouldn't be caught dead doing anything else but ministry.

One may wonder, then, what happened to Joe W., or why today's minister so often comes to the Center ill at ease. The symptoms vary from case to case, but fretfulness, listlessness, boredom, and anxiety are not uncommon. Neither are loneliness, frustration, depression, and despair.

In this chapter, I invite you to look at (1) the causes of ministerial dis-ease[1], (2) the signs of its presence, and (3) its prevention and cure.

The Roots of Ministerial Dis-Ease

Let's begin with the obvious: *the nature of ministry itself.* At the Center for the Ministry we talk with ministers about their ministry. Even if we limit our discussion to the local parish pastorate, the ministry has always been a general practice profession, and it remains so in this age of specialization. One young pastor offered a medical analogy. She said, "I'm expected to be an obstetrician, a pediatrician, a gerontologist, an internist, a cardiologist, a radiologist, a psychiatrist, and a neurosurgeon. Then, on Sunday morning, I'm to put together some sort of combination of forensic medicine and anesthesiology!" She was finding this an impossible task in a time of pseudoenlightenment when parishioners think they know quite a lot about each of these "ministerial specialities." You might argue that overly high self-expectations are at the core of this minister's frustrations, but the general practice of ministry does make multifaceted demands.

The nature of ministry is such that it is, at best, difficult to tell when one is doing a good job. It is a sufficiently ill-defined kind of work, and it varies so much from community to community that measurement of performance and achievement is extremely difficult. When life was simpler for the minister, perhaps as recently as the 1950s, most might have agreed that an increasing budget and burgeoning membership were valid criteria for measuring ministerial success. But our culture and the whole religious scene have changed so much that even these criteria may no longer be helpful. For instance, a parish pastor may be doing a heroic, profitable, and perfectly splendid ministry in a church that grows smaller year by

[1] I am using "dis-ease" to connote ill at ease, discouraged, or disenchanted. In this sense, dis-ease is incipient burnout, if burnout is defined as true existential exhaustion (usually manifested clinically as depression).

year. It is tragic when confusion about achievement in such a situation results in the minister's feeling smaller.

Second, there is *the nature of the Christian faith.* Attorneys have regard for great lawyers and their teachings, but those who practice law are not personally dedicated to those outstanding leaders. Physicians take the Hippocratic oath, but, if they are captured at all, it is by a compassion for life, not by a personal devotion to Hippocrates. In ministry there is One who is central to our faith. He is the supernatural model. We are not only captivated by his teachings; we are devoted to his person. Unfortunately, the Christ emerges in many ministers' experience as more of a slavedriver than the gentle Master who is known in meditative moments because ministers find it hard to imitate this perfect model. Who doesn't feel small and unworthy in comparison with Christ? The mistake many ministers make is getting fixated in those feelings of smallness and unworthiness.

Third, we need to look at *the nature of the person who answers the "call."* That is, we must be aware that some of the root causes of ministerial dis-ease lie in the minister himself or herself, that is, in the minister as a person. Our data at the Center for the Ministry suggest that there are certain types of people who are more responsive than others to the call of ministry. The characteristics which render these persons receptive may also render them more susceptible to certain dis-ease. Among the characteristics most frequently found among the Center's ministerial clientele are these: idealism, inner-directedness, creativity, sensitivity to interpersonal interactions, vulnerability, concern for social issues, keen self-awareness, high intelligence, ability to communicate effectively, sympathy, and passivity (or passive ways of dealing with aggressive tendencies if there is any aggression showing clearly).[2] Superficially, ministers as individuals vary from this characterization. However, there seem to be some bedrock similarities.

It is these similarities that suggest ministers' vulnerability to certain dis-ease. Passivity or noncompetitiveness is often an indicator

[2]Among the instruments used to measure personality functioning at the Center for the Ministry are the Minnesota Multiphasic Personality Inventory, the Rorschach Inkblot Test, the Sixteen Personality Factor Questionnaire, and the Myers-Briggs Type Indicator. I have also borrowed data and perceptions gathered at the Center for the Ministry in Wellesley Hill, MA. I am particularly indebted to the Reverend Irene E. Lovett for her helpful collation of material and her penetrating insights into the nature of ministers and ministry.

of the fear of getting out of control; many ministers are very controlled and controlling. Creativity and concern with social issues may reap frustration or disappointment. Sharp sensitivity and self-awareness render many ministers overconcerned about how they are being received, how they come across, whether others accept or reject them. A strong conscience, high moral values, and zealousness tend to exacerbate these traits. A combination of these factors plus the passionate nature of the Christian gospel itself makes it very difficult for clergy to divorce their ministerial identity from their personal one.

Idealism and intelligence can contribute to unrealistic expectations of self and others. There are so many ministers who drive themselves unnecessarily and even mercilessly that it seems safe to say there are tendencies *within* as well as without that foster ministers' feelings that they aren't doing enough, no matter how much they do. As I noted earlier, the boundaries of ministry are so wide and amorphous that it is easy to overload oneself with work; the nature of the task "loads the dice." However, all too often ministers make little consistent effort to organize the job in order to do what is realistic and comfortably endurable. Instead they walk about heavy-laden, guilt-ridden, conscience-stricken. Then, to the burden of guilt-based anxiety (or even acute depression), they add dwindling self-confidence or self-esteem.

At the Center for the Ministry we routinely administer tests of general ability.[3] These test results indicate that there are almost no ministers of merely normal intelligence. They are nearly all above normal! In most cases, they are easily capable of postseminary graduate work, such as an academic doctorate, and there is little doubt that they could readily succeed in any number of so-called secular occupations. Yet very often ministers' self-estimates are far below what the scores show. This is not false humility. Ministers genuinely underestimate themselves.

The Symptoms of Ministerial Dis-ease

The signs of dis-ease with ministry are many, and they vary depending on the individual, the personal family situation, and the work setting. I caution the reader not to seize upon one or two of

[3] Terman's Concept Master Test, the Shipley-Hartford Vocabulary and Abstractions Scale, and often the Wechsler Adult Intelligence Scale, which deduces a "full scale I.Q." indicative of general ability based on eleven sub-tests of specific abilities.

the following symptoms as conclusive evidence of what I am calling "dis-ease." However, the following are some of the symptoms regularly noted at the Center for the Ministry:

- overweight
- absence of regular physical exercise
- failure to take vacations or a regular day off
- chronic tension, anxiety, stress
- overbusy yet bored; trouble with time management
- declining sexual appetite
- a feeling of disenchantment or cynicism about the church and its ministry
- lack of playfulness, loss of a sense of humor
- lack of close friends or confidantes
- waning self-confidence
- bouts with depression
- preoccupation with financial worries
- fear of what the future holds
- low resistance to illness and fatigue

The above are in random order, and positives can effectively offset negatives. For instance, if the minister is fortunate enough to have an intimate, playful, sexually active marriage, this can provide self-assurance, allay future fears, and give relief of tension. The symptoms given above are closely interrelated; so it is likely that the minister with quite a number of these symptoms (for example, six of the above) is on the path that could lead to serious dis-ease or ultimately to burnout.

Not long ago, a young minister participated in one of the Center programs. He had graduated with high honors from both college and seminary, working his way through. Now married and with two small children, he was in his second pastorate, a small blue-collar congregation in a declining neighborhood. His idealistic expectations and evangelical zeal had left him, and in their place were many of the symptoms of dis-ease described here. At the end of his three-day Career Development counseling program, he wept with joy at the rediscovery of his innate sense of worth. He also decided to retool for a career outside of the professional practice of ministry. He is a gifted person. His exodus from formal ministry may not hinder him from a full life or from contributing significantly to the church-at-large. However, his leaving is surely a loss to his denomination and ministerial colleagues.

Prevention or Cure: Toward Wholeness

How does the minister avoid these pitfalls? How does she or he move toward a healthier ministerial career than the kind I have been talking about? How does one prevent ministerial dis-ease or overcome it and move toward wellness?

The theologian Paul Tillich defines faith as the courage to accept acceptance,[4] and by that he means acceptance of God. *Courage.* The final part of this chapter needs to be cast in the context of such a courageous faith—the courage to accept acceptance.

Rather than talking about what other ministers ought to do, I want to speak now in the first person. I am by no means immune from ministerial dis-ease. If I am to get well or stay well as a minister, I must accept God's acceptance of me, others' joy that I am who I am, and my own inborn love of self. I must give myself permission to be me. I must allow myself to take God's offer of abundant life (John 10:10*b*) seriously. In that firm hope of God's abundance I may be able to take charge of my life and move intelligently and intentionally toward self-actualization, and self-fulfillment.

I cannot presume to say what that may mean for each of my fellow ministers. We are not all alike: some are men; some are women; some are celibate; others are married, and so on. I can, however, state what the courage to accept acceptance means to me. In so doing, I hope my peers will draw their own inferences and apply them courageously to their lives.

In brief, I believe ministerial wholeness has to do with ordering my use of time, energy, talents, interests, and skills in keeping with my personal needs and values and the work God gives me to do. Here are my personal priorities:

1. **Self-Care**—One can scarcely lead another in his or her growth beyond one's own maturation. The Good News of the gospel falls on deaf ears when couched in a "bad news" package. Only out of the overflow of the wellspring of my own being can I share living water. At the risk of offending some colleagues, this means, for example, not being fat, sloppy, and ill-groomed. It means maintaining vibrant health in *every* fiber of my being—staying well physically, mentally, emotionally, socially, recreationally, sexually, spiritually, maritally, and parentally.

[4]Paul Tillich, *The Dynamics of Faith* (New York: Harper & Row, Publishers, Inc., 1957), pp. 16-17.

I truly believe that the typical traits I have described as common to most ministers are neither good nor bad per se. They simply predispose persons to answer the call, and the ministry is a lifework which permits these traits to be assets rather than liabilities. But when a conscience is so oversized that it cannot allow appreciation of oneself and one's assets, or it causes an individual to be so unyielding in point of view or so relentless in mode of behavior that a person will not listen to others or permit any other way of life than one's own, this trait becomes a handicap. Or when sensitivity becomes so finely tuned that one is too thin-skinned to take criticism, that person is in trouble. Or when passivity takes over so that one cannot embrace anger as a normal part of human expression, depression usually results. Or when one's self-discipline and self-control become so lackadaisical that even the outward physical appearance is repulsive, then that minister's impact value is diminished.

How good are you, then, at self-care? How expert at dealing in kind, gracious, forgiving ways with yourself? How motivated at seeing to it that your body, mind, heart, and spirit are fed a healthy dietary regimen?

2. **Tending My Primary Relationship**—(The unmarried minister may want to skip this point and turn to priority 3 or 4 below.)

Each of us needs to decide what comes first, second, third, and so forth, given our particular life situation. Second only to self-care, for me, is the feeding, watering, and occasional pruning of my primary relationship—my relationship with my wife. I need to take the initiative in seeing to it that she and I continue to will to grow in love with each other.

Courtship is the most frequently ignored task among the ministers I've counseled at the Center for Ministry. I have marvelled at how often ministerial marriages can accurately be characterized as "two people living alone together." I frequently suggest to couples that they establish a date night—set aside a block of time for the exclusive purpose of romancing each other—and that they make this time inviolate. Many have reported great benefits from putting this simple idea into practice. However you do it, courtship is crucial to a growing marriage. Courtship is fun, but it also takes effort.

3. **Parenting**—At the Center we are privileged to counsel not only ministers and missionaries and their mates, but also their sons and daughters. It is sad how frequently these people wistfully wish

their parents had taken time to be their mentors, playmates, and friends. For me, parenting is the third highest priority, right behind self-care and courtship of my mate. It is an investment.

Another kind of parenting should be taken seriously by ministers, namely the mentoring of one's spiritual children, particularly ministerial candidates and others who show promise as future church leaders. Whether I am talking about biological offspring, adoptive sons and daughters, or spiritual children, as a minister I am a parent. Parenting and modeling what it means to be a parent are functions of my pastoral identity. I want to pay attention to the quality of my parenting. Only self-care and caring for my life mate matter more.

4. **Close Friends**—The fostering of close relationships with confidantes is another often neglected or misplaced activity. Women in ministry or unmarried ministers tend to do a better job of maintaining friendships than do men or marrieds in ministry, but few do this as well as their health requires. Especially among male ministers, I fear that comradeship has become a lost art. Loneliness and fear of peers is woefully common. As well as I can piece it together, the rationale goes something like this, expressed by a minister who came to the Center, "I did not want to seek spiritual direction from unspiritual people. I was afraid to share my growing inertia with my fellow ministers. I had been taught not to confide in parishioners. I was distrustful of mental health professionals. I tried pouring my heart out to God and got no answer. I finally spilled it all to my wife as best I could, but she only could listen and add my burden to her own heavy load." This minister then tried to "go it alone." By the time we saw him at the Center, he was clinically depressed.

The most satisfying relationships in my life, the ones that have sustained me during times of deep trouble, have not come to me automatically nor because they sought me. If they are mine, it is because I have sought them, wooed them, and won them. If they remain mine, it is because I persist in courting them. I want these close friends for the richness they bring to life. I need them because of the load I sometimes carry as a minister and especially because of the heavily interpersonal nature of my work. I need them within reach—a local phone call away. Letter writing is too slow when I am needy, and long distance calls are expensive.

I am astounded at the many ministers who, by their own admission, have *no* close friends. The result is personal and professional malnutrition.

5. **Professional Improvement**—Growing as a professional is somewhat like riding a bicycle. When one stops moving forward, one falls. Many ministers do not read, except as is minimally necessary for sermon preparation. Some become stale or archaic because schooling is something they *did,* not something they *do.* In the next chapter, William Malcomson shares a number of excellent ideas regarding continuing education for ministry. I urge the application of these ideas. In a sense, continuing one's education is another kind of self-care, but it is more than that. It is moving toward true professionalism. It is enhancing one's strengths for efficiency and effectiveness. It is learning to do best what one likes best to do.

6. **Doing Ministry**—Doing the work God gives me to do and doing it well—that is surely of high importance in my response to God's call. However, I place it sixth among my personal priorities because I believe that is where it belongs. I also believe that, if my first five priorities are cared for, my ministry will get done—skillfully, wisely, well. It will get done because I have taken loving care of my every need so that I am ready to nourish others efficiently and happily.

So you are an idealistic minister? Good! One can scarcely be a Christian, much less a Christian minister, without valuing the ideal. Let us temper our idealism with a healthy awareness of reality.

So you are sensitive and sympathetic and somewhat passive? Good! Who but the sympathetic and sensitive can heed, and keep on heeding, the injunction to "feed my sheep"? Who but the somewhat passive could get along with the typical church constituency?

There is in the Book of Exodus a passage which reads:

> Moses said to the LORD, "Oh, my Lord, I am not eloquent, either heretofore or since thou hast spoken to thy servant; but I am slow of speech and tongue." Then the Lord said to him, "Who has made man's mouth? Who makes him dumb, or deaf, or seeing, or blind? Is it not I, the LORD? Now therefore go, and I will be with your mouth and teach you what you shall speak." But he [Moses] said, "Oh, my Lord, send, I pray, some other person" (Exodus 4:10-13).

Moses had the dis-ease: an over-big conscience, a poor self-image, a hypersensitivity to failure, unrealistic and idealistic notions about ministry. Yet history records that he accomplished quite a bit for his Lord.

In the Bible, holiness has something to do with wholeness, and wholeness has something to do with holiness. I doubt whether a minister today can be one without the other. I also doubt that we ministers will *stay* well unless we have full measure of both wholeness and holiness.

Recommended Reading

Augsburger, David W., *Anger and Assertiveness in Pastoral Care.* Edited by Howard J. Clinebell and Howard W. Stone. Philadelphia: Fortress Press, 1979.

Glasser, William, *Positive Addiction.* New York: Harper & Row, Publishers, Inc., 1976.

Goldberg, Herb, *The Hazards of Being Male: Surviving the Myth of Masculine Privilege.* New York: The New American Library, Inc., Signet Books, 1977.

Gould, Roger L., *Transformations: Growth and Change in Adult Life.* New York: Simon & Schuster, Inc., 1979.

Hauck, Paul A., *Overcoming Depression.* Philadelphia: The Westminster Press, 1973.

———, *Overcoming Worry and Fear.* Philadelphia: The Westminster Press, 1975.

Lakein, Alan, *How to Get Control of Your Time and Your Life.* New York: The New American Library, Inc., Signet Books, 1973.

Lowen, Alexander, *Depression and the Body: The Biological Basis of Faith and Reality.* New York: Penguin Books, 1973.

Pelletier, Kenneth R., *Mind as Healer, Mind as Slayer.* New York: Delacorte Press, Delta Books, 1977.

Rediger, G. Lloyd, *Coping with Clergy Burnout.* Valley Forge: Judson Press, 1982.

Salzman, Leon, *The Obsessive Personality.* New York: Jason Aronson, Inc., 1968.

Warlick, Harold C., Jr., *How to Be a Minister and a Human Being.* Valley Forge: Judson Press, 1982.

Self-Directed Education—A New Day for Learners

William L. Malcomson

Chapter 2

A good friend of mine recently participated in a career assessment event. After he had finished, I asked him if he now knew more about his career goals and how to achieve them. He said that he did, but that I had not asked him about what was for him the main benefit of his experience. The crucial bit of wisdom that he now carries around with him is that he is responsible for his own life. He is not totally dependent on peers, parents, and those in authority. He is "in charge." The burden and the responsibility to decide how to live his life is on his shoulders and not on the shoulders of others who act on his behalf. He has begun to experience the "new day."

It has taken me a long time—over forty years—to realize what my friend has learned. I can take charge and intentionally plan my life. Not that I can do this fully, of course. None of us can include in our plans all of the unexpected events which often make life frustrating but also exhilarating. However, I can be much more intentional than I had ever realized. I do not need to wait passively for someone to find the time to tell me what it is all about. No one can live my life for me. No one is going to offer me *the* job in the world for me. No one is going to open up opportunities for me which are tailor-made for me. I can take charge, make my own mistakes, experience my own fulfillment.

The "Old Day" in Education

Is the following account indicative of your experience as well as mine? Throughout my years of formal education, I thought of education as receiving what others believed I needed in order to function in this society, learning what I needed to know in order to be an educated person, acquiring enough information so that I could get a meaningful and well-paying job, and earning enough academic degrees to insure future job flexibility. I believed in the wisdom of adults, in the advice of authorities, and in the expertise of my professors.

It was not until I moved into graduate work that I began to take greater charge of my education, to become more self-directed. However, even then I was dependent on the financial aid which was offered by the educational institution. In fact, I chose the particular graduate school that I attended primarily because it offered me a scholarship. I earned a degree in a field in which I was not all that interested but which was more interesting to me, so I thought, than any of the others that were offered in that particular school. It did not occur to me to try another school in which I could do what I wanted to do. I was experiencing the "old day" in education.

It might be well to focus briefly on the *assumptions* that appear to underlie the "old day" in education. Perhaps we can be helped to understand the significance of our experience in the past if we look at the foundations on which this view of education was based.

1. Education is passive, rather than active. We are to learn what those who know tell us we need to learn. "Teachers know best."
2. *Formal* education or "schooling" is equatable with education. Formal education ends at a particular time—when we have finished school.
3. Education is future-oriented. It is preparation *for.* Indeed, education is done in a time of preparation. It is oriented toward a job, a vocation, a calling. Education is a means toward an end.

There is also often a theological assumption behind this view of education. That assumption is that there is a God who knows fully what you and I need in order to live and work. This knowledge which God has is, in turn, revealed to us through adults, authority figures, teachers, ministers, and others. We are to receive this revelation gratefully and in humility. In the educational arena we are to learn from teachers and textbooks. Discussion groups are "fun," but the problem is that what we can learn from fellow students is so eclipsed by what we can learn from God through experts that the former seems like "shared ignorance." It is the authoritative "others" who know, not *we* who are students.

I remember that during my college days a very insightful person quoted to us a bit of wisdom that was quite prophetic—"Never let education interfere with your bull sessions." She was ahead of her time—out of touch with the then current educational and theological assumptions.

The "New Day" in Education

Those were the old days. There is a new day coming. Indeed, the new day in education has already come, but not everyone is aware of it. My job in this chapter is to help you to become aware. If you are already aware, I would like to help you to take advantage of this new day, and enter into the joys of self-direction.

Having stated the assumptions which underlie the old day in education, let me picture the assumptions of the new day.

1. Education is active, not passive. We learn according to our own needs, goals, and interests. We tell educators what we want to learn. "Learners know best."
2. Education is lifelong. It begins with birth and does not end until death. Formal education can occur at any time during one's lifetime, depending on one's needs. No academic degrees are terminal.
3. Education is present-oriented. Education is often short-term preparation for specific goals as well as long-term preparation for future goals. Further, the purpose of education is as much, if not more, for the enhancing of life than it is for the achieving of career goals.

As we come into the new day in education, we realize that we can develop our own uniqueness, our particular talents. A key word is "intentionality." We intend to set goals, to reach those goals, and to set new goals. Other key words are "plan," "negotiate," "assert," and "make happen." Theologically speaking, I am coming to believe that God wants us to be active.

God has created each of us as a unique human being with a specific set of talents, interests, needs. No one of us is interchangeable with any other. God has given me *my* mind, *my* body, *my* spirit, *my* background, *my* family, *my* autobiography. God wants something different from me than from other persons. Who I am, what I do, who I am becoming, is my gift of *me* to God, my gift of *me* to other persons, and my gift of *me* to me. God's gift encourages my giving. How dull it would be if we were clones—not only dull for us but, I would reverently imagine, dull for God as well!

When I talked about the old day, I suggested what it was like and then stated its assumptions. Having already stated the assumptions inherent in the new day, I would now like to talk about the characteristics of the new day. I will do this through sharing some experiences I've had which convinced me that a new day is here in education. These experiences, in one form or another, are ones that you can have as well. Many of the events which I shall describe included both laity and clergy.

Educational Needs Assessment

One of the most important events in which I have participated, both as a peer participant and as a leader, is that of an educational needs assessment. This is a technical term for a process that treats the participant as a whole person who wishes to plan his or her educational program in the light of that reality. In the process one analyzes the roles that one plays personally, professionally, or both; the skills that one brings to these roles; the knowledge one has; and one's unique personality characteristics. Then, after considering all of these elements, one tries to plan for one's education.

For example, I might affirm that a significant role which I play is that of facilitator of groups. I also have particular skills in listening and analyzing what I hear. I possess a fair amount of knowledge of group process. One of my major personality characteristics is empathy. Do I want to expand my skills, knowledge, and experience in the facilitating of groups? If I do, then I might look to a local educational institution for courses and/or workshops in that field. I might also join with others in my profession who have similar skills and knowledge and work out ways in which we can learn together. My educational needs assessment has led me to read books, take classes, and commit myself to tasks which have helped me in my chosen profession and in the enhancing of my life. I had not known that education could be as exciting as it has been since I have determined what I am doing and why I am doing it.

The program in educational needs assessment which I feel is the best in the country is conducted by Dr. Thomas Brown of St. Louis, Missouri.[1] If you have an opportunity to participate in one of his seminars or in a seminar conducted by persons who have been trained by him, I would strongly urge you to do so. There are other kinds of educational needs assessment and other formats for such assessment, but I feel that Dr. Brown's is the best.

Career Assessment

Akin to and often allied with educational needs assessment is career assessment. The American Baptist Seminary of the West in Berkeley, California, has developed a program for those who are interested in pursuing its Doctor of Ministry degree. In this program an educational needs assessment, a career assessment, and an introduction to the degree program are combined in a creative and exciting way.[2] It is difficult to do an adequate job of assessing your educational needs unless this is done along with an analysis of your career path and your goals for your vocation. If you cannot do these together, I would encourage you to do all within a short space of time.[3]

A variant of career assessment can be experienced in what is called an "intentional growth" seminar. Dr. Mark Rouch, a pioneer in the field of continuing education for ministry, conducts such seminars in a center at Lake Junaluska Assembly in North Carolina.[4] These events include a lot of peer feedback, consultation with ministerial colleagues, and development of possible scenarios for one's future. Having co-led one of these seminars, I know that it can be an exhilarating and valuable experience. Some of the best features of this format is that it is long enough to accomplish something—

[1]Write to Dr. Brown at Career Planning Centers of America, Inc., 8420 Delmar Boulevard, St. Louis, MO 63124.

[2]For more information write to Dr. Leland D. Hine, American Baptist Seminary of the West, 2515 Hillegass Avenue, Berkeley, CA 94704.

[3]For further information: In the east write to Dr. Connolly Gamble, Division of Christian Higher Education, American Baptist Churches, Valley Forge, PA 19481. In the midwest write to the Reverend Henry I. Fox, 20 North Ashland Avenue, La Grange, IL 60525. In the west you can write to me at the Center for the Ministry, 7804 Capwell Drive, Oakland, CA 94621.

[4]Dr. Rouch's address is Intentional Growth Center, Box 546, Lake Junaluska, NC 28745.

nine days—and is relaxing and unhurried enough to give participants time to think about what is happening.

The Importance of Shared Learning

One of the most encouraging signs in the lives of ministers these days is their willingness and eagerness to learn from one another. Not long ago I participated in a retreat for ministers—senior, solo, and associate pastors—in which they functioned as teachers to one another. The topic was "worship." Each of the ministers designated as a resource person did a presentation on worship from his or her perspective and experience and asked for feedback, affirmative and negative. It was a fascinating experience for me to see how much the ministers appreciated receiving from one another. No one was an "expert." I felt that the participants were remarkably free from the usual jealousies and competitiveness that is current among professionals in any field.

I might add as a footnote that in the western states we have developed a directory, which we call the Resource Bank, which lists the names, addresses, resource skills, and references for over one hundred ministers and spouses in the American Baptist denomination who reside in the thirteen western states. The idea of this Resource Bank is to encourage those who want to learn from peers to do so and to stimulate those who plan educational events and administer educational institutions to draw upon the resources that are in our midst.[5]

The new day in education can involve us in educational events that cut across racial barriers. Because of my particular job, I have been privileged to participate in events that have taken me out of my usual mono-racial (white) environment—and placed me in situations where I learned from Hispanic, black, and Asian leaders.

As a white person, I know that I am different from my black brothers and sisters. I am discovering—particularly with my Christian brothers and sisters who are black, Hispanic, Asian, Native American, or whatever—that I am not an alien. I am also discovering that I can learn from these brothers and sisters. I can learn not only about their cultures but also about the Bible, the doctrines of faith, the meaning of church life, and so on.

[5]If you would like to receive a sample copy of the current Resource Bank, write to me at the Center for the Ministry.

Not long ago, a black minister and I were talking about inviting white ministers to attend a continuing education event which was directed primarily to black ministers. He said, "The whites won't want to come to an educational event with classes and such." I asked, "Why not?" "Because," he responded, "most white people don't believe that black people can teach them anything in the way of content." If you are white, I would encourage you to seek out opportunities to participate in such events. I believe that you would discover that you are welcome. Those of us who are white do not often realize that persons of other races are not always as threatened by us as we are by them.

A fascinating new possibility for significant education in our day lies in the process of "futuring." Here one really becomes intentional about one's education, for what a person is asked to do is not only to look at what might happen in the future, based on past trends, and to learn how to adjust but also, and more important, to look at and to develop his or her own "preferred futures."[6] I recently attended a conference in Los Angeles, sponsored by my denomination, in which the participants focused on preferred futures. Clergy and laypersons were present at the event. There was communication and mutual growth across racial and theological lines. We focused together on the future of the church's mission. The fact that such an event can occur within the Christian community should be encouraging to us.

One of the major tenets of contemporary adult education is that truly educational events are developed with the leaders in collegial relationship with the potential participants of the events. It would be difficult for me to number the planning teams on which I have served which included as members those persons who would participate in the event being planned. We were not planning *for* but planning *with*. The people were taking charge of their own education. Let me give you a specific example of such planning.

In the western states my denomination sponsors what is called a Western Continuing Education Biennial. We have been doing this since 1976. Every two years we hold a continuing education event for ministers and spouses. On the planning teams for these events

[6] A good book along these lines is E. B. Lindaman and R. O. Lippitt, *Choosing the Future You Prefer* (Ann Arbor, Mich.: Human Resource Development Associates, 1979).

are parish ministers, minister's spouses, denominational leaders, and employees of educational institutions as well as lay persons who have expertise in areas that are of particular concern to ministers and spouses (stress management, working with volunteers, time management, and so on). These teams send out questionnaires to potential participants prior to the planning. The questionnaires gather data about areas of interest and concern. The teams then look over this data, add their own insights, and develop goals for the events and formats designed to meet these goals. Each team recruits leaders, conducts the event, and then helps the participants to evaluate the event after it is over. Thus the data-gathering continues throughout the event and afterward. I have gone into some detail in describing this process because I feel that it illustrates in a graphic manner the points which I have been making regarding the new day in education.

The New Day in Theological Education

What does what I have been saying tell us about the education of ministers of Jesus Christ? Is the new day in education a new day for ministers? Is it a new day in theological education? Yes, it is.

Theological education, like all education in the new day, is lifelong and should become intentional and self-directed. It is not confined to the days spent in a seminary setting. There is a reason beyond the obvious financial one why seminaries are moving more and more into extension education. It is because solid and relevant theological education cannot end with a Master of Divinity program. Ministers are not preparing for their ministry by spending time in a theological institution. Rather, they are engaging in but one stage of the lifelong process of learning. In seminary they are learning how to learn. They are learning how to sift the significant wheat of wisdom from the less significant chaff of information. Theological education is a lifelong process.

Theological education is not only for professional clergy. A number of seminaries are developing what are sometimes termed "paraministerial programs." These are geared for lay persons who want to dig more deeply into the Bible and Christian thought than is usually possible in the life of the local congregation. Some theological institutions and denominational educational programs are experimenting with clergy and laity learning together as peers.[7]

[7] If you are interested in learning more in terms of formats, descriptions of events in the areas of clergy and laity learning together (experiential theologizing, spiritual growth, etc.), please write to me at the Center for the Ministry.

Negotiation is a key to education in the new day. A minister in the new day should learn how to negotiate with seminaries and other institutions regarding his or her needs for theological education. When we assess our needs, set goals, and then work out ways to meet these goals, we will find it necessary to negotiate with educational institutions. My advice to ministers is never to assume that an institution is tied down to what is stated in the catalog (even the current one) or what may be said by an educational administrator in an initial conversation. It is usually helpful to talk first with someone in the office of extension (adult or continuing) education. I would not go first to an admissions person or a registrar, and deans are usually too busy to see you right away.

Do not be intimidated by persons in educational institutions. They are fellow professionals and they want to please. You have clout in the community and it is to their professional advantage to negotiate with you. If you do not see what you want, ask about the possibility of the institution's offering in the future what you do want. You may be told that there is not enough interest in the topic. Then you could offer to talk to persons you know and check out the interest.

Perhaps you are already taking a class, and it is not going in the way you feel would be most helpful to you. Do not be afraid to negotiate with the instructor—explain that you would be helped to a greater degree if certain changes were made. Then state your desired changes. If the instructor is not an insecure person, she or he could very well be pleased to learn that there is a student in the class who is interested enough to ask for a change.

You may be interested to learn, incidentally, that many theological institutions in our day are open to negotiation regarding the granting of credit for professional experience. If you desire an academic degree and have completed some but not all of the educational requirements, you might look into this possibility.

Theological education in this new day is both professionally helpful and life-enhancing. Wouldn't it be exciting if ministers studied theology or church history or the New Testament for *fun?* What if we were to study for the pleasure of it, for the enhancing of life—not only because we are preparing sermons or developing a course, but also because we want to, because such study adds to the meaning of our lives both personally and professionally? Who said that lifelong education for ministers had to be confined to the traditional disciplines of the theological curriculum? So-called "secular" fields of knowledge can be life-enhancing and often professionally helpful as well: photography, auto mechanics, gardening, behavioral sciences, management, geology, and on and on.

It may be age creeping up on me, but I sometimes wish that I were starting over in my educational pilgrimage. What a fantastic time to be alive, to experience education as self-directed, negotiable, and based on my unique needs, talents, and interests, and to realize that so many people stand ready to help me as I seek to realize more fully the gifts that God has given me—the gifts that I can give to others and thus return to God as my offering.

Recommended Reading

Gross, Ronald, *The Lifelong Learner.* New York: Simon & Schuster, Inc., 1977.

Houle, Cyril O., *Continuing Learning in the Professions.* San Francisco: Jossey-Bass, Inc., Publishers, 1980.

Kemper, Robert G., *The New Shape of Ministry: Taking Accountability Seriously.* Nashville: Abingdon Press, 1979.

Knowles, Malcolm S., *Self-Directed Learning: A Guide for Learners and Teachers.* Wilton, Conn.: Association Press, 1975.

Lenz, Marjorie, and Shaevitz, Marjorie, *So You Want to Go Back to School.* New York: McGraw-Hill, Inc., 1977.

Rouch, Mark, *Competent Ministry: A Guide to Effective Continuing Education.* Nashville: Abingdon Press, 1974.

This Matter of Money

Terry L. Burch

Chapter 3

As we sat talking, he recounted in casual fashion the bills that they owed. His plan was to consolidate them all with a loan from a finance company. His wife interrupted from time to time to explain with embarrassment why it had seemed necessary to charge so many items. I recalled in silence a magazine article I had once read about people who owe more in monthly installments on indebtedness than they receive in monthly income.

The scenario for their future was not much brighter. He had served a string of small churches on modest salaries. They had always lived in parsonages, and the question of where they would live in retirement had either not crossed their minds or was buried beneath a host of more immediate concerns. I knew from experience that low salaries mean low-pension contributions and also reduced Social Security benefits. Somewhere the whole picture had to be changed. The time to start was now.

Out of the many professional responsibilities of the minister, an important one is this matter of money control. Money control is tougher for ministers than most other professionals because ministers' incomes are comparatively low. Yet they are often expected to live, dress, and drive like other professionals. They are bombarded with the same advertisement blitz as other Americans and are urged to "Consume! Consume!" In addition they are solicited to give money by two or more schools which they may have attended and are expected to provide a model of stewardship in giving to the church. Ministerial careers and marriages are often wrecked by careless steering through financial waters. The purpose of this chapter is to give ministers and their families some suggestions to help them in the voyage.

Often it is the minister's spouse who is better able to handle money. That's all right. What is important is that a couple agree on who does this task and to make sure that it is done well.

Maximize Your Income

If you are going to accumulate something for emergencies, retirement, or things you simply want to do, it is obvious that your income has to be greater than your expenses. (Don't scoff. Millions of Americans do not see the logic of this argument.) You may contend that, as someone who is "called," salary is not your most important concern and that, at any rate, the church is already doing its best to provide for you. But *is* the church doing its best? Or is it coasting along with the good bargain that it has, and are you afraid to present the church with your needs and its responsibility as an employer? It is amazing how some ministers will jeopardize their future and their families' welfare under the guise of protecting the church.

Increasingly, though, ministers are taking responsibility for their own financial well-being. They have educated their official boards to review the pastoral budget each year. They have made certain that professional expenses, such as automobile and convention expenses, are fully reimbursed by the church. If their income is not adequate to meet their family's needs, they have faced the hard questions of whether the spouse should work, or the pastor take on additional jobs or look for a church that can pay an adequate salary.

In most denominations the pension in retirement is commensurate with the salary earned during active years. Low salaries mean low pensions. Making sure that the church is doing its best in compensating the pastor now can bring dividends later in retirement. I have, on occasion, talked with a retired pastor who is belatedly angry over his own neglect in church after church to deal with this issue of a fair salary.

Have Adequate Insurance

Hearing about a neighbor who just made a "killing" in real estate or about a friend who bought a stock which doubled in a year can cause "visions of sugar plums." But are these investments for you? Maybe later, but not yet. Financial counselors caution that you first make sure that you have adequate insurance. Ask yourself these questions: How much would my family need if I should die right now? How much would I or my family need if I became disabled right now? Are we adequately insured against illness, fire, automobile accidents, and legal suits? The answers to these questions will vary from one family situation to the next and from one period of time to the next and will determine how much insurance you should have.

In general, life insurance, although good *protection,* is not a good *investment.* Most insurance agents are eager to sell whole life insurance where part of the premium builds up equity. It is better to purchase term insurance, which is pure protection, and invest the premium you save in a savings and loan bank. Whole life insurance, *is,* however, a form of saving (a conservative one) and many people will pay these premiums who would not otherwise save.

Incidentally, if you do already have ordinary life insurance, it is often wise to borrow up to its cash value. The insurance company will usually charge you 5 percent or 6 percent interest on the loan, but you can invest the loan in a savings and loan bank, credit union, or money market fund which pays a higher interest rate. Then you reap the difference in the interest rates, rather than the insurance company. It is a financial angle worth pursuing.

Pay Yourself First

My point here is that if you do not take a specific and regular amount out of your paycheck for savings, you probably will not save at all. Most people assume that savings comes out of the surplus which is left when all other needs are met. The trouble with this assumption is that there seldom is any surplus. Somehow the "needs" expand to meet the income or even to exceed it. Make the amount you put into savings realistic—not too little, but also not too much. Regularity is probably more important than the amount.

Where shall you save? Volumes are written in answer to this question, and I shall not duplicate them here. Most financial advisors recommend first that you have an emergency fund of from three to six months' income which you can get hold of in a hurry. Remember, this is not a "slush fund," and you will have to resist the temptation of defining "emergency" too broadly. Savings and loans banks and credit unions are good places to keep this fund. Both insure your savings, and credit unions usually pay a little more interest. At certain periods, money market funds pay even higher rates. They invest the money very conservatively, and some even allow you to write checks. The money is usually instantly available. They are advertised in financial periodicals.

Let's say that you are adequately insured against life's contingencies and that you have saved your emergency fund. You now qualify as an "investor." There are no "hot tips," however, as to where everybody should invest. There are available stocks, bonds, and money market funds as well as real estate, real estate investment trusts, and second trust deeds. Look over the financial page of your local newspaper, or peruse a copy of the *Wall Street Journal* to get an idea of the range of your options.

Who, then, can survive in this jungle of competing offers? Certainly not you and I. At this point we have to trust specialists who spend most of their working hours assessing the potential markets of corporations, the demographic moves of populations, guessing whether the prime interest rate is going up or down. The average minister has neither the time nor the inclination to pick this stock and to reject that one. It is better to ask someone you know and trust for advice, such as your banker. If you have a lot of money to invest, however, beware of well-meaning friends who have a "deal" on which you cannot possibly lose. Remember that, generally, the higher the potential return, the more risky the investment.

Do not invest in anything so risky that it will disturb your sleep. Personalities differ, and some people are more willing to take risks on "high flyers" than others. If you are conservative, you will want to keep your money where the principal is secure: savings and loans banks, bank certificates of deposit, U.S. government securities. There is, however, a danger in being too conservative. If your investments are earning less than the rate of inflation, they are in fact being eroded in their purchasing power. You might want, therefore, to invest in several areas of differing risk to avoid "putting all your eggs in one basket." Again, experts feel that the older you are, the less risk you can afford. The young, on the other hand, have more opportunity to recoup their losses.

Beware of Debt

Mention has already been made of the persuasive power of advertising. Appeals are made to our most base instincts to buy love, status, and happiness. Creditors are falling all over each other to extend us credit. Strangely, the more credit you have, the more you are likely to be offered. The end result for too many Americans, including some ministers, is that they slide easily, almost imperceptibly, into debt. Actually, most of the items you need or want can be bought with cash. Part of each month's income needs to be put away toward the purchase or replacement of "big ticket" items.

There are two purchases which usually justify credit: a house and a car. Both purchases should be made after careful research to make sure that you are making a wise investment, not buying a dream. Then you should shop for credit the same way that you shop for anything else. Banks, savings and loans banks, loan companies are all in the business of selling money. The Truth-in-Lending Law should help you to compare interest rates, but you still need to make sure that you understand all the conditions of a loan. When it comes to a house, it is wise not to sign anything—an offer to purchase or a loan agreement—without an attorney's recommendation. It is too big a commitment.

A word of caution: avoid leaving unpaid balances on credit cards. The interest rate is usually 18 percent a year. Make it a practice not to charge any more than you can pay off at the end of the month.

Avoid Taxes

Please note, I said *avoid* taxes, not *evade* them. To evade them is against the law, but no one is required to pay more taxes than the law requires.

Ben Franklin said, "A penny saved is a penny earned." Actually, because of income tax, a penny saved is worth more than a penny earned because it has not been reduced by federal and state income tax. All of which brings us to the importance of tax-excluded income and tax-deferred savings. For ministers, the housing allowance is an example of the former. Your denominational pension plan is an example of the latter.

Tax-Excluded Income

The Internal Revenue Code allows ordained ministers to exclude from reported income whatever it takes to provide a home. The value of a rent-free parsonage is excluded. If the minister is given a housing allowance instead, that is excluded as well as whatever is spent for utilities and major furnishings. The church must designate the amount to be considered as housing allowance in advance of the tax year. The maximum that the minister can exclude is the least of the following three: the amount of compensation which the church designates as housing allowance, the amount actually spent for housing, or the rental value of the house with furnishings plus the cost of utilities. Before you take the housing allowance, you will want to make sure that you meet your denomination's standard of ordination. If you are purchasing a home, what you are doing, in effect, is building up equity (ownership) in an appreciating piece of real estate and doing it all with tax-excludable dollars.

If you are in a parsonage, all is not lost. You can still buy a house and rent it out. While you cannot cover its cost with a parsonage allowance, there are attractive income tax benefits in depreciating the value of the house for tax purposes while year after year it is usually appreciating in value. Then, by the time you retire, you have built up some cash value in a house. I am sympathetic with those who tell me that they had to live in parsonages all their active years and now cannot afford a house. In my experience, however, those who live in parsonages have more disposable income than those of us who are supporting a house. Some of that extra income could be set aside year by year into a nest egg that will eventually purchase a home.

Tax-Deferred Savings

Internal Revenue allows ministers to put up to 20 percent of their includable compensation from the church into a tax-sheltered annuity. It is tax-sheltered because it is not reported as income now but is reported when you receive it in retirement as an annuity, a lifetime income. Your denominational pension plan qualifies as such an annuity. You would do well to become familiar with this plan and to determine whether it, along with Social Security, will meet your needs in retirement. If it doesn't, you usually can put away money on a tax-deferred basis over and above your present pension contributions. Your pension plan may offer you a program for doing this. If not, a commercial insurance company can sell you a tax-deferred annuity. The formula for determining how much income you can defer from tax is complicated, and you had better make sure the agent properly calculates it.

Speaking of Social Security, it is basic to all retirement planning. Ordained ministers are automatically included in Social Security but must pay the tax on a self-employed basis at the same time that they pay their income tax.[1] Too many ministers overlook the fact that Social Security includes survivors' and disability as well as retirement insurance. It probably will be your largest source of income in retirement. At the same time, the benefits to your survivor(s) could be sizable if you become disabled or die before retirement. Pick up a pamphlet at a Social Security office and read about the potential benefits. Every few years you should send in a form postcard available at post offices and Social Security offices to request a report on your earnings. If Social Security has made any mistakes, you will have time to notify them to make corrections.

Start Now

Your spouse and you ought to dream occasionally about retirement—what you will do, where you will live. Then constantly monitor your anticipated income in retirement. If it will not be enough, now is the time to start a savings program, preferably tax-deferred, to supplement it. "Next year" never comes. Ideally, your goal should be to own a house before you retire. That way you will not be spending a large share of your limited income for rent or mortagage payments. Very few people in retirement feel that they saved too much. Many regret that they did not save more.

Start taking responsibility for your own financial future now, and happy savings!

Recommended Reading

Holck, Manfred, Jr., *Making It on a Pastor's Pay.* Nashville: Abingdon Press, 1974.

Porter, Sylvia, *The New Money Book.* New York: Doubleday & Co., Inc., 1979.

Rifenbark, Richard K., *How to Beat the Salary Trap.* New York: Avon Books, 1978.

Tobias, Andrew, *The Only Investment Guide You'll Ever Need.* New York: Bantam Books, Inc., 1979.

[1] A minister may opt out of Social Security within two tax years of ordination, but the exemption is based on conscientious objection to government-sponsored insurance.

Ad-Ministering in the Eighties

Leroy H. Sandberg

Chapter 4

If I were to characterize ministers in America today from a management point of view, that is, looking at the minister as the chief executive officer of a corporation, I would have to say that most ministers enjoy giving pep talks to their employees on Sunday but really hate to run the business during the week. This characterization is not intended to minimize the importance of preaching. Preaching is extremely important from both a biblical and practical perspective. It is to say, however, that most ministers do not see themselves as administrators/managers and thus neglect an equally important aspect of ministry. The day by day and year by year overseeing of the operation we call the local church is all too often seen as some necessary evil that has to be done to survive and not as the fulfilling of one's call. Somehow, administration is not seen to be as "spiritual" as preaching, evangelism, counseling, or even the art of pastoral visitation.

Ministers who have been fortunate enough to escape the "administration is non-spiritual" snare may have been caught in the trap of the anti-institutional attitude of recent years. This attitude surfaces in such statements as "Don't waste your time on the institution or the organization" or "Let the organization run itself" or, again, "Let lay people do it." The managing or administrating facet of ministry in the local church has not been a high priority in training or in practice for a large segment of the present-day clergy.

Today's minister, however, must be an administrator of the corporation, that organization or institution we know as Old First Church of Podunk. For if the church is to fulfill its purpose on earth, it must know what that purpose is—not just in theological or biblical terms, as important as these are, but also in terms that make sense to the people in the individual congregations and to the ultimate consumer of the church, the world.

The newly elected first woman bishop of the United Methodist church typifies many clergy when she ranks her new duties by saying "third is the nitty gritty of administration. 'You do it to get it over with.'"[1]

To assist a congregation in finding its purpose and to work with that congregation in carrying out that purpose on a day by day, week by week basis is the task of management. And I would contend that this is the task of ministry. The two are the same. *To minister is to administer.* It is so obvious that it is often overlooked—the word "administer" itself simply means "to minister." Yet we in the church have left the word and the function to so-called secular institutions.

Few persons, if any, would equate the church with only the clergy. The church is also made up of those designated laity for whom there appears to be an ever-growing appreciation and emphasis. Any local congregation is a complicated mixture of persons, paid and volunteer, trained and untrained, sick and well, rich and poor, and a host of other categories in varying combinations.

The point is that this strange mixture we call the Body of Christ must have order and direction. This giving of order and direction is the task of ministry and is what administration is all about. Administration is not shuffling papers, or something that a person does when "promoted" to a denominational job. It is a high and noble calling.

I have said to pulpit committees charged with the responsibility of bringing a pastoral candidate to their congregation that the minister in today's world is expected to be an expert in more areas than persons who work in any other profession. But increasingly I am

[1] Jean Caffey Lyles, "An Improbable Episcopal Choice," *The Christian Century,* vol. 97, no. 26 (August 13-20, 1980), p. 780.

convinced that an understanding of what administration is and the willingness and skill to put it into practice are necessary for any minister to bring to a congregation today.

Administration is a big subject. There are a number of books available on the more limited area of church administration. The purpose of this chapter will be to point out the importance of administration in fulfilling one's ministry in the eighties. To that end, let us explore three myths about administration that are generally accepted by a large number of clergy for a variety of reasons. The myths are that: (1) administration is not "spiritual"; (2) administration is not very important; and (3) administration is not interesting.

Myth #1: Administration Is Not Spiritual

When I graduated from seminary more than twenty-five years ago, I must admit that I had the idea or impression that administration was somehow a necessary evil. It had to be done, but one should do as little of it as possible so that one could get on with the real work of ministry, namely, preaching, teaching, and evangelism. Administration was not what I was "called" to do—certainly it was not my understanding of my call at the time. One did not join the Rotary Club as a community leader or even because one enjoyed the fellowship or the food, but in the cause of evangelism—in hopes that someone might be brought into the church through that contact. Likewise, planning was not that important. If one were doing the right spiritual tasks, somehow everything would come together. If persons "got right with God," the budget would be raised, and if they had "enough faith," the new sanctuary could be built.

Look for a moment at one specific area of administration—delegation. To delegate responsibility to others is both a necessary and a sound administrative practice. It is also good theology. In fact, most of us in the church have tried to recruit, train, and utilize lay persons in the life and mission of the congregation. Unfortunately, much of this recruiting is done on the basis of "if you loved God more," you would and could do the specific job. No doubt we all need to love God more, but that club has not proved to be the most effective way of obtaining lay participation in the life of the church.

How are persons motivated to assume responsibility in a voluntary organization like the church? Position, recognition, tangible rewards, and the meeting of other individuals' needs are a few of the motivators that an administrator recognizes and uses to accomplish the recruiting task. The goal—participation in ministry—is the same no matter what the motivator. Yet it is possible that we are not using all the tools available to us in the church to accomplish the kingdom's task.

I can recall that in the churches I served, my administration was mechanical. I worked at writing or rewriting church constitutions. I tried to trim the "deadwood" from the membership rolls. I dutifully did the every-member canvass. The latter was expedient, the former somehow made sense. I did a lot of things that I had been taught to do, that had been done previously, and that were expected in the churches I served.

I failed to see at the time that planning, evaluating, and working with boards, committees, and the organization of the church in an effective manner and to some meaningful purpose was both ministry and administration. At the time I had not learned that, had I been a better manager, I also would have been a better minister and that I would undoubtedly have come closer to accomplishing the more "spiritual" goals to which I was dedicated. I was trained in theology; I was not trained to be a manager. I have learned through experience, reading, and study in administration that being a better church administrator makes my theology more effective and efficient.

My experience may not have been yours. My experience may not have convinced you that administration is indeed spiritual and that it has a legitimate place in ministry. Thus, a brief look at the biblical basis for this position may be helpful. Not a great deal has been done in the biblical study of administration. One of the few available books on the topic, Kenneth Gangel's *Competent to Lead,* aroused my interest in this area.[2]

The apostle Paul tells us that gifts are given to persons for "the work of ministry" (Ephesians 4:11-13). Ministry is *work;* it is a task; it does not just happen. In a similar passage, Paul indicates that God has appointed persons for various tasks in the church (1 Corinthians 12:28). The first tasks listed are very familiar—apostles, prophets, teachers. Then Paul lists helpers and administrators, according to the Revised Standard Version. The King James translation of "helpers" and "governments" does not clarify the concept. Modern translations are better, e.g., giving "ability to help others" and "power to

[2]Kenneth O. Gangel, *Competent to Lead: A Guide to Management in Christian Organizations* (Chicago: Moody Press, 1974), pp. 19-21.

guide them" *(The New English Bible),* and, again, "to help others" and "to direct them" (Today's English Version).

The word translated "administrators" in the Revised Standard Version (the Greek word is *kubernesis*) has behind it the concept of guidance, literally steering or piloting. This word and a variant of the same root—*kubernetes* (steersman) or *kubernao* (steer)—are used in the Septuagint in Proverbs and Ezekiel (Proverbs 1:5; 11:14; 24:6; Ezekiel 27:8, 27, 28). *Kubernetes* is used in Acts and Revelation (Acts 27:11; Revelation 18:17); in Acts the word is translated "captain." Gangel cites Gerhard Kittell in his *Theological Dictionary of the New Testament* to point out the all-inclusive role of the captain of a ship. The captain is responsible not only for steering the ship but also for knowing the ship's capabilities, the water currents, and the nature and directions of storms. My visit to the bridge of the aircraft carrier USS Enterprise a few years ago made this passage and concept very real to me. Administration is having at hand all the possible knowledge about the situation and accepting the responsibility to see that the task is carried out.

Another word often translated as "rule" in the King James Version more accurately may be translated as "administer" or literally "to take the lead." This word is used in Romans 12:8, for example, and is translated in the Revised Standard Version as "he who gives aid" (see also Titus 3:8, 14; 1 Timothy 3:4; 5:17; 1 Thessalonians 5:12).

Other New Testament concepts such as service or ministry, stewardship, and servanthood all have implications of administration/management for the pastor/manager of today. Therefore, one cannot take administration lightly from a biblical point of view. Nor can the task of ministry neglect employing all available concepts to accomplish a common goal.

Myth #2: Administration Is Not Very Important

If an average American corporation functioned and operated its organization as many average American churches operate, it would have gone out of business long ago. I have made this condemning statement to a number of pastors' groups and have not been challenged. The corporation depends upon the sale of its product or services for its success. The bottom line of the annual financial report is the generally accepted measure of success in a business. The church, however, has no such generally accepted criteria for measuring success. Statistical indicators, such as attendance, membership, and budget, are often used as illustrations of success when they are increasing but are rationalized as false, unspiritual indicators when they are declining. Churches have faithful members who continue to give their support financially and otherwise long after a church ceases to be a viable institution. Perhaps this is as it ought to be. As good stewards of all that is entrusted to us, we in the church have the responsibility to manage that trust wisely.

To measure success in the church is not easy. To measure failure is even more difficult. It is not easy to grapple with what ministry is in any given situation and to ascertain whether it is taking place. That is, at least in part, what management/administration is about and why it is so important for ministry in the coming years.

Let's explore a second reason why administration is so important. In recent years a great emphasis has been placed on organizational development, human relations, and small groups. Various terms have been used to describe the importance of the interaction between persons in a variety of settings and situations. While not minimizing the place and importance of interpersonal relationships, I would simply add that it is equally important to plan and carry out the training and effective use of such skills in the total program of the church. In other words, for what purpose do we seek good interpersonal relationships? Too often we hope to end up feeling good about each other and instead we end up feeling bad—and have accomplished nothing. The pastor, as the chief executive officer of the corporation, must see that every aspect of organizational life is put into perspective and coordinated into the life and mission of the church.

I am not denying the divine nature of the church or the ministry, concepts with which we are all familiar. I am saying that there are a number of functions carried out by a pastor—such as planning, organizing, staffing, directing, coordinating, and budgeting—that are identical to those functions of a secular manager or executive in a corporation or business. The leader who ignores these functions will be in difficulty. If clergy have any "divine weight" to throw around, it ought to be in the area of leadership. I believe in prayer, but not prayer alone. It takes prayer and a lot of hard work to administer the earthly organization we call the church as well as prayer and a lot of hard work to minister in that divine institution we call the church.

Look at staff relationships as one specific example. I know of a pastor who was doing a good job in an above-average-sized church. He felt he wanted and needed an associate. A seminary graduate was hired by the church. The associate lasted less than two years and shortly after that the pastor was also forced to leave. Good staff relationships do not just happen. It takes training and a considerable amount of preparation, particularly for those entering into a staff situation for the first time, to create and maintain good staff relationships. I have said to many pastors and associates alike that good staff relationships are difficult at best and they go downhill from there.

The pastor, as the chief executive officer, has and must assume responsibility for ministerial staff relationships. The hiring, supervising, and firing of ministerial staff ought not to be delegated to a board or committee although there may well be a working relationship with a board or committee. Many ministerial staff problems develop because pastors are either not willing or are not prepared to assume this responsibility.

The area of staff relationships, however, obviously includes all employed staff—musicians, clerks, and custodians as well as ministers. It includes volunteer staff as well as persons on boards and committees. The principle with the non-ministerial staff is the same even though the hiring and firing dynamic may be different. Much of this responsibility can be carried out through delegation. But, given the complexity of society today and the church as a part of that society, someone must oversee the church organization and the staff relationships. That someone is the pastor.

How a pastor carries out that responsibility makes a difference, and this is a third reason why administration is so important. Historically, the "how" goes back to the time when the minister, because he or she had more education than the congregation and "had God on his or her side," ran the church in the manner of a benevolent dictator. In recent years there has been a trend toward the other extreme, where the congregation participates in all of the administrative functions and the pastor is only an enabler in the process with little, if any, responsibility for what happens in the life of the church.

Both extremes exist today. Much of the leadership in the fast-growing ultra-conservative churches is of the former type while the more traditional mainstream churches tend to have more participative leadership. In between, a large number of churches are not sure what kind of leadership they want or why. Also, large numbers of clergy do not know how they want to function nor do they care. Consequently, a great deal of frustration on the part of congregations and clergy alike is due to the administrative style issue not being taken seriously. And pastors who are only theologically trained are not ready or able to deal with this non-theological factor any more than are their congregations.

I am no longer convinced that there is one best style of administration. A great deal depends on who the pastor is and how he or she functions best. The pastor needs to know that. Then, also, the pastor need not always function in the same style. Participation is desirable within a long-range planning committee, but when the building is on fire, one cannot afford the luxury of a committee meeting—someone must yell "Get out! The building's on fire! Go that way!"

However one functions at any given time or over a period of time, that person must know how she or he is functioning and why he or she functions in that manner at that particular moment, and then be responsible for functioning in that manner. One of the most demoralized groups I ever witnessed was a church-related organization whose executive insisted that he was functioning democratically when in reality he was often a less-than-benevolent dictator behind the scenes.

Robert Golembiewski of the University of Georgia has a very simple rule of thumb that can be very helpful. A good manager should not make more than six decisions a year on behalf of his or her organization. If a manager makes more than six major decisions, chances are that the additional decisions could and should have been made by someone else or by the organization as a whole. If a manager makes no decisions, he or she may well not be doing what he or she is being paid to do. There are times when a decision must be made that only the manager can and should make and for which he or she should be held accountable. If as a pastor/manager I limit myself to six decisions concerning my congregation, it is not likely I will make the decision what color to paint the broom closet unless that decision cannot be reached in any other manner.

The fact that we live in a complex and diversified society is another reason why administration is an important concern. This complexity and diversity is reflected in church congregations. No leader can make everyone happy all of the time. I have seen pastors completely frustrated because they could not please the entire congregation. I have also seen pastors charge off on a white steed caring little if they pleased anyone. The pastor/manager must keep both a sufficient popular base of support and his or her principles at the forefront of his or her thinking. And the pastor must be skilled in handling the conflict when the two are not in accord. My observation is that many pastors leave the ministry not because they have lost the "call" but because they fail at this point of management.

There is one final factor in the case for the importance of management/administration in the church. That we are living in a time of rapid change has been said so many times we revolt at hearing it again. But it is true. While some congregations are essentially the same as they were fifty or seventy-five years ago, many congregations find their environments entirely different today from what they were even five years ago. The sociological and environmental setting for every congregation is unique to that church. It is imperative that churches in the eighties know who they are and where they want to go. It is the responsibility of leadership and the manager to assist the church or congregation in that important process. It is the task of the church to proclaim the Word, to be sure; but guiding the church in deciding where, when, how, and to whom the Word is proclaimed is the task of management. It is important that these questions be answered by every part of the Body of Christ. The pastor/manager must lead the church in searching for answers to these difficult questions.

Myth #3: Administration Is Not Interesting

Admittedly, if one's concept of administration is limited to opening the mail, putting out the church newsletter, and buying the tissue for the restrooms, the fires of administrative interest may well go out—if indeed they were ever lit. But, on the other hand, if one can grasp administration as the carrying out of the task of ministry as I have described it here, then I would venture to say the fires may be rekindled. Increasingly in the coming years the church must have pastors who are managers, who are trained and willing to assume the responsibilities of the chief executive officer for the corporation which is the church.

Most readers will be familiar with the theological concepts of the pastor, with the priestly and prophetic functions of ministry. Without questioning for a moment the validity of the theological images and the role of the minister, let's look at the role through secular glasses just for a change of perspective.

While corporation laws vary from state to state, most states, if not all, provide for churches to be registered by the state as a corporation. There are good reasons for a congregation to do this and undoubtedly most congregations have become incorporated under the laws of the state where they exist. Again, most, if not all, state laws require a corporation to have a board of managers or trustees that is responsible for seeing that the corporation's purpose is carried out. Many board members of incorporated religious institutions are unaware of this responsibility.

Most corporations through their legal boards hire staff to carry out their goals and purpose. In this sense, the church is no different. The pastor is hired by the corporation (the congregation) to see that its goals and purpose are carried out. The pastor who is not willing or prepared to carry out these responsibilities in the eighties will be in trouble; if she or he finds a congregation of a like mind, not much more than "church keeping" will be going on.

Some will insist that administration is necessary in the big church but is unimportant in the small church. If anything, the reverse is true. In the small church everything is generally more limited—financial resources, lay leadership, program possibilities, and community standing and influence. The small-church pastor will probably not have adequate secretarial help, if there is any at all. The pastor of a small church must be a better administrator, in most instances, than the pastor of a larger church. And we must keep reminding ourselves that small churches are not few and far between; most major denominations have at least half of their churches in the small-church category.

Another area of administration that should raise the interest of the pastor is money. Few churches are without budget problems and yet few pastors give much creative attention to finding financial resources for the undergirding of the mission and the outreach of their churches. Too many pastors see the budget as a necessary evil; yet they feel that raising money is far beneath their calling, even though their own salaries depend upon it.

Many say, "If we get their hearts, we'll get their pocketbook." That may be true, but with the rising costs of fuel, ultilities, and supplies, pastors need to give more attention to getting the most out of their churches' present dollars and to finding additional dollars.

In many instances, the money is available, but it is being siphoned off by those who know how to raise money for causes good, bad, and everything in-between. Managing money is not a simple task, and there are no easy answers. For the pastor to acknowledge the fact that the budget is within his or her responsibility is a step in the right direction.

Administration is also interesting because it gets the pastor involved in how to spend his or her time: How do I spend my time? How ought I to spend it? Where does my family fit in? What about time for my own personal interests? These are questions that can have only increasing importance in the coming decade. To look at these questions honestly and without feeling guilty can be very exciting and freeing.

I have referred to responsibility a number of times. It can be exciting to work through this subject with a congregation. The congregation, the official boards, and the pastor and staff each have responsibilities for which they are held accountable. To be held accountable means that the responsibilities must first be defined. Yet they are often assumed to be understood and taken for granted or carved in stone and thus unable to change with changing situations.

Pastors should write out their understanding of their role and the role of the official board. In turn, the board should write out its understanding of its role and that of the pastor as they see it. The pastor and the board may be surprised when they compare the descriptions. Yet this process is but a single step away from an ongoing process of evaluation of the church and its leadership. The dialogue and communication that such a process necessitates between pastor and people can be extremely beneficial to the overall effective ministry of a congregation.

Finally, administration can be exciting if it is seen as a vital and necessary part of one's ministry. If planning, evaluating, budgeting, working with boards and committees, and all the other phases of administration can be seen as a means of fulfilling the pastor's calling and of attaining the church's and pastor's mutual goals, and if these activities are accomplished with increasing regularity, new excitement can be experienced by ministers in the eighties.

We who have been theologically trained often respond to the administrative issues discussed in this chapter only in theological or biblical terms. But these same issues also need to be answered in terms comprehendible to persons in the pew and the community. Peter Drucker says that the customer never buys a product. The customer buys the satisfaction of a want; he or she buys a value.[3] The church of the eighties needs to ask: What is our business? Who really are our customers? Where are they? What is the value or what are the values they are seeking? What value or values do we have to offer? In seeking answers to these questions, all of us have the task of ad-ministering.

Recommended Reading

Anderson, James D., and Jones, Ezra E., *The Management of Ministry.* New York: Harper & Row, Publishers, Inc., 1978.

Campbell, Thomas C., and Keierson, Gary B., *The Gift of Administration.* Philadelphia: The Westminster Press, 1981.

Gangel, Kenneth O., *Competent to Lead: A Guide to Management in Christian Organizations.* Chicago: Moody Press, 1974.

Hutcheson, Richard G., Jr., *Wheel Within the Wheel.* Atlanta: John Knox Press, 1979.

Kilinski, Kenneth K., and Wotford, Jerry C., *Organization and Leadership in the Local Church.* Grand Rapids, Mich.: The Zondervan Corporation, 1973.

Richards, Lawrence O., and Hoeldtke, Clyde, *A Theology of Church Leadership.* Grand Rapids, Mich.: The Zondervan Corporation, 1980.

Rudge, Peter R., *Ministry and Management: The Study of Ecclesiastical Administration.* New York: Methuen, Inc., Tavistock, 1968.

Sayles, Leonard R., *Leadership, What Effective Managers Really Do and How They Do It: Effective Behavioral Skills.* New York: McGraw-Hill, Inc., 1979.

Schaller, Lyle E., and Tidwell, Charles A., *Creative Church Administration.* Nashville: Abingdon Press, 1975.

White, Robert N., ed., *Managing Today's Church.* Valley Forge: Judson Press, 1981.

[3] Peter F. Drucker, *Management: Tasks, Responsibilities, Practices* (New York: Harper & Row, Publishers, Inc., 1974), p. 61.

The Minister's Spirituality

Robert L. Charpentier and William L. Malcomson

Chapter 5

One of the major religious trends in the late seventies and early eighties is an emphasis on spirituality. This emphasis has been strong in Roman Catholic circles for a long time. It is fairly new among Protestants. At a recent convention of the professional society of those who program continuing education for ministers, the topic was "Spiritual Formation—A Continuing Education Task." Most of the resource persons were Roman Catholics and most of the conferees were Protestants. Many of the conferees came with a bit of "fear and trembling," wondering if they would be led into an experience that they didn't really want, or if the topic of spiritual formation was too limited and even a bit esoteric. On the contrary, they were happily surprised to be ushered into what many perceived to be a whole new world that offers hope for a more deeply fulfilling life and ministry.

The authors of this chapter symbolize in their own lives what is happening among ministers in our time. Bill Malcomson is a Protestant of the American Baptist tradition, to whom much of this emphasis is very new and different. Bob Charpentier is Roman Catholic and so has been involved for a long time with that rich spiritual tradition. Thus, our sharing in this chapter reflects the dialogue which is currently going on in the ecumenical arena.

Malcomson

I have always associated the word spirituality or the phrase "spiritual formation"[1] with regular prayer times, reading the Bible daily, and living according to a discipline of devotion. Some guilt has developed on my part because I did not do any of these tasks regularly. Also I have felt that I might be missing out on something that is worthwhile. But, frankly, I have often been "turned off" by speakers who have touted the benefits of a devotional life as nothing short of miraculous.

In my middle years some needs have emerged in me. For example, I am coming to terms with my mortality. I seem to have a need to "leave my mark" before I die. With this need I have experienced a growing fear of loss—loss of parents, spouse, children, friends. In fact, very recently two professional associates, one slightly older than myself and the other a few years younger, have died, and I am thinking, "This year everyone is dying." Secondly, I am admitting my need for solitude. I have a strong desire to be alone for some period each day and for longer periods from time to time. My developing desire is to learn to become a friend to myself. Finally, there is a growing realization in me that psychotherapy can be of help to me in my marriage and my parenting, but that I also need to focus directly on my faith, my relationship with God, and my deep religious needs. Psychotherapy does not do that for me. Therefore, I have a sense that some of my deep needs are not being addressed while others are.

As I have become aware of these needs I have sought help in meeting them. One of the activities in which I have engaged is reading the works of Henri Nouwen as well as listening to tapes of his talks on solitude and silence. Also I have become involved in the experiential theology movement which has helped me to affirm my ability to theologize—to verbalize my faith stance—out of reflection on my own experience rather than a heavy reliance on the works of professional theologians. I have done some talking with Roman Catholic leaders about spiritual formation. With one of these leaders, I have co-led a spirituality workshop for American Baptist ministers

[1] A term common in Roman Catholic circles; the concept is perhaps more familiar to Protestants as "spiritual growth."

and laity. I have also done some counseling with a spiritual director. I have made a personal retreat, spending about two weeks by myself, concentrating on my own spiritual development.

At this stage of my pilgrimage I feel that I have learned the following:

1. A person needs to develop a program of spiritual formation that fits her or him. This requires a lot of trial and error. For some, a regular devotional discipline is helpful; for others, such as myself, that doesn't work. I have discovered that it has been helpful for me to take some personality tests. The results gave me some insight into what I can expect of myself in terms of my particular personality configuration and so helped me develop my personal program. (Tests such as the Myers-Briggs Type Indicator and the Sixteen Personality Factor Questionnaire have been useful.)

2. For me, the following disciplines are of help.

   a. *Keeping a journal,* but not doing it slavishly (I don't have to write in it every day of my life). I need to be at times brutally honest with myself in my journal; so I am writing for me, not for publication.

   b. *Making visits to a spiritual director.* Again, I do not do this regularly, such as once or twice a month, but intermittently as the need is felt.

   c. *Going on periodic personal retreats.* I feel that once a year for a minimum of seven days it is important for me to be by myself with no stated agenda. I also try to be by myself for the equivalent of at least one day or more a month.

   d. *Attending experiential theologizing events.* Sometimes I help conduct such events; at other times I am an ordinary participant.

   e. *Leading spiritual growth workshops.* This helps keep me honest in terms of my own spirituality. Also I find it very exciting to find out how other people are experiencing spiritual formation.

   f. *Doing my praying more honestly.* This means, in part, that I do more "cry from the heart" types of prayers. I say what I feel to God whether it sounds sophisticated or not. I don't worry about the words, only about being truly open to God and to my experiencing of God.

g. *Being truer to myself.* It is very important for my spirituality that I follow my intuition. In fact, this is the key to my spiritual formation. I try to do what I feel I need to do, want to do, and am called out of the depths of my being to do. I believe that God speaks to me best through my intuition. This involves becoming friends with *me.* It also means celebrating God's creating and sustaining of my uniqueness.

What I am talking about is not a patterning of my life after some other spiritual guide, nor am I suggesting that you pattern your spirituality after mine. What I would encourage you to do is to find your own way rather than to assume that someone else's way will or should work for you. Spirituality is not a method; it is a way of relating to God, yourself, and others—a way of approaching life. I do not believe that God wants us to feel guilty because we are not someone else, but I do believe that God wants us to feel guilty if we are not true to ourselves.

Charpentier

My early spiritual development was typical of a Roman Catholic child of French Canadian ancestry growing up in a small New England town. In my family, emphasis was primarily on devotional practices. Reciting the daily Rosary and attending Sunday Mass with my family, serving as an altar boy, attending the local parochial school where daily catechism lessons and prayers were routine, participating in parish feasts and many other church-related activities were all part of my early experiences. As I reflect on those early years, spirituality was primarily something one *did.*

Even in seminary in my early twenties, spiritual practices or "devotions" were a very important part of the daily routine. Daily Mass, Rosary, a set time for private prayer and meditation, daily "examination of conscience," weekly Confession, regular "visits" to my spiritual director, and conferences on spiritual themes continued to be the "stuff" of spirituality. For the most part I accepted this approach unquestioningly.

I recall reading a book, in a course on spirituality, called *The Soul of the Apostolate* that helped me to identify what had been my approach to spirituality. It has been a long time since I read the book, but, as I remember, my thinking went something like this, "This is sort of a filling station approach—you do spiritual things to fill the tank so that you can push on in the big bad world out there." Something was missing! I would soon discover what it was.

A typical day in the parish was very different from the ordered life of seminary. "Father, Mrs. L. needs a Mass card." (Mrs. L. knows that this is my meditation time.) "Father, the president of the youth group wants to know if you could talk with her on the phone about the beach trip." (Sally knows that this is my spiritual reading time.) "Mrs. P. just called to say that her father has taken a turn for the worse and wants to know if you could come right over." (There goes my visit to my spiritual director.) My seminary spiritual formation had not prepared me for this! What happens if one can't get to the filling station?

In those early years of ministry I missed the regularity of spiritual exercises that had become routine in seminary. I felt guilty when I couldn't complete my daily spiritual activities. I remember talking with my spiritual director about these concerns. His advice still makes sense to me, "Do the best you can. You have to find your own way." I gradually learned that he was talking about a more integrated style of spirituality, one that would reflect the active life-style of a parish priest.

The first really practical help I received came—interestingly enough—from a Protestant source: a Clinical Pastoral Education (CPE) progam. CPE challenged me to integrate my spirituality (mostly the "head tripper" variety) with my pastoral role. Naturally, I had heard of the need for so doing during my seminary years and from various spiritual directors. But this was different. In the program someone read my daily reports and gave me feedback. In addition, daily small-group interaction with fellow ministers provided a context for active learning. I was impressed with the care and concern of Protestant clergy who, for the most part, had few or no "filling stations" in their daily lives and yet appeared to be very concerned with ministry and spiritual growth.

The years of doctoral studies brought still more changes in my life. I moved from the East to the West coast. I became a full-time student again and a part-time minister. Eventually my personal life-style changed radically when I decided to marry. This change forced me to rethink and restyle my ministry completely.

During these years perhaps the most important thing I learned had to do with my spiritual style. With so many changes occurring, I realized that my spirituality had to reflect my personality and life-style. As an "active" person I felt my spirituality needed to reflect an active life-style. If spirituality was to be meaningful *for me,* it really had to reflect who *I* was. (Quite a change from my early years when spirituality had to do with something one *did*—not something one *was*!)

Now, in my late thirties, I think I have finally begun to integrate an "active" spirituality into my life-style. My style of prayer is primarily active. I try to make what I do a prayer whether it's getting ready to meet with a difficult client or jog or swim after a particularly busy day. For me, talking to God from the heart and sharing where I am at the moment is important: in the counseling office, "Lord, help me to say the right words . . . the healing words . . . your words . . . your healing touch"; or at the poolside, "Thank you for the warm sun, the good feelings that come from a hard swim." I'm not saying I do this all the time, nor am I suggesting that my style should be yours. Rather, it seems important that each of us develops his or her own spiritual style. In the same way, my choice of worship reflects my style. I prefer worship in a small group where I can be involved and challenged.

Though I prefer an active spirituality, from time to time I like to withdraw, to "retreat" (shades of the filling station!). A half-hour of meditation helps me to be more receptive to ten minutes of reading from the Bible when my day has been unusually active. On the other hand, twenty minutes of yoga before fifteen minutes of Bible reading helps me to wake up in the early morning or after a period of primarily mental activity. Occasionally I like to withdraw for longer periods of time: a day, a weekend, sometimes a week to a quiet setting (I like to backpack in the Sierra) for more prolonged and intense "alone" time. Again, this works for me. It may not for you.

Ultimately, discovering what works for *you,* identifying *your* particular spiritual style are what this chapter is all about. Bill and I have shared some of our journeys. We feel strongly that spirituality needs to come out of who we *are* rather than what we *do.* We invite you to think about this. We also invite you to take a "spiritual inventory." We hope that some of the questions will challenge you to think about your spiritual life. You may or may not want to score your "Spiritual Life-style."

Spiritual Inventory

Directions: Check the appropriate answer box for each question.

	Yes	No
Do you pray?	☐	☐
Do you read the Bible regularly?	☐	☐
Do you have a spiritual advisor or guide?	☐	☐
Do you have regular quiet times for meditation or reflection?	☐	☐
Do you give money or time to community needs?	☐	☐
Do you consider yourself free of racial prejudice?	☐	☐
Do you ever take stands based on your religious beliefs?	☐	☐
Do you seek out educational experiences with a religious or spiritual theme?	☐	☐
Do you view your spiritual growth as related to your psychological and biological growth?	☐	☐
Do you ever disagree with the "official" stance of your minister or church?	☐	☐
Do you attempt to integrate your spirituality with your personal life?	☐	☐

Scoring:	Two points for "Yes"; zero points for "No."
0-8:	Improvement needed
7-14:	Doing well
15-22:	Excellent

Recommended Reading

Benson, Herbert, *The Relaxation Response.* New York: Avon Books, 1975.

Edwards, Tilden H., *Spiritual Friend: Reclaiming the Gift of Spiritual Direction.* New York: Paulist Press, 1980.

Leech, Kenneth, *Soul Friend: The Practice of Christian Spirituality.* New York: Harper & Row, Publishers, Inc., 1980.

LeShan, Lawrence, *How to Meditate: A Guide to Self-Discovery.* Boston: Little, Brown & Company, 1974.

Nouwen, Henri J. M., *The Way of the Heart.* New York: The Seabury Press, Inc., 1981.

Fit or Misfit: The Minister's Spouse

John R. Landgraf

Chapter 6

I have known men who have left the professional ministry because of their wives. I have known others who stayed in the ministry to please their wives. In the years ahead, I suspect that certain ordained women will also leave the ministry or remain in it because of pressure from their husbands. Thus, it is appropriate to ask, "Where does the minister's spouse fit?" or, more specifically, "What is a person's role in the church if married to the church's professional leader?"

Because the data presently available on spouses of women in ministry is not extensive enough to justify generalization, I am confining myself to talking about ministers' wives—non-clergy women married to male ministers. My discussion is addressed to clergymen, especially to men who are parish pastors. In order to speak to the question "Where does the minister's wife fit?" I will first talk about who she is, next about some of the problems she faces, and finally about the basic options available to her as she views herself and lives her life.

Who Answers the "Call" to Minister's Wifehood?

For several years I have been privileged to counsel with ministers and their spouses. Across the United States there are about fifteen counseling centers doing the same kind of work,[1] and the counselors in this network of centers frequently compare notes to benefit from each other's experience. Based on this data, here is a portrait of the typical minister's wife:

> She is a sensitive, caring, modest woman who is brighter (measurably more intelligent) than the stereotypical female in our culture. She has high moral and ethical standards, and she values conflict-free interpersonal relationships above such entities as money, social status, or power. She is quite self-conscious and often overcontrolled; that is, she keeps her impulses in check and tries to behave in harmony with what she feels her role or reputation requires. She is somewhat overly feminine in the sense of a willingness to assume burdens (whether or not they are rightfully hers to assume) and even to place herself in situations wherein she will be imposed upon. In comparison with other women in today's society she is often less assertive about her own values and opinions.

I do not mean to imply "good" or "bad" in the above. These traits can be a help or hindance, depending on how one handles them. Perhaps you are married to a woman who does not approximate the above sketch, and that is certainly all right. For many ministers' wives, it does more or less fit; and for those to whom it applies, this personality package is often more of a bane than a blessing.

I have said, in effect, that the typical minister's wife is more feminine than the typical woman. Well, would you believe that the typical male minister is considerably more feminine than the typical man? That's right. Briefly, let me sketch him:

> He is an idealistic, inner-directed man who is socially perceptive and keenly sensitive to interpersonal interactions, particularly as to how he is received in an acceptance-rejection way. Typically, he reflects such characteristics as superior intelligence, astute self-awareness, concern with social issues, and the ability to communicate ideas clearly and effectively. He is also likely to have a highly developed superego or conscience and to be relatively passive (or passive-aggressive, if there is aggression showing clearly at all) and non-competitive as well as sympa-

[1] The centers referred to are affiliated with the Church Career Development Council, 475 Riverside Drive, New York, NY 10027. Descriptive literature is available by writing to this address.

thetic and overcontrolled, or at least fearful of ever becoming out-of-control.

Again, these traits may be assets or liabilities depending on how you, as a male minister, deal with them. Unfortunately, most minister husbands of these women, through no fault of their own, are little help in counter balancing their wives' traits. When speaking before a group of ministers' wives, the point I try to make is that *they should not expect help from their husbands which their husbands may be unable to furnish.* Ministers may find either that they are too close to the situation to deal with it objectively or that their own personalities stand in the way of handling the situation well. To put it to ministers directly, if your wife is to formulate goals and strategies for becoming healthier and happier than she is, she will need to look beyond you for resources. But before further discussion of that issue, I want to turn to some of the dilemmas currently confronting ministers' wives.

Typical Problems of Today's Minister's Wife

Married to somebody who tries, as most ministers do, to be "... all things to all [people] that [they] might by all means save some" (1 Corinthians 9:22), the minister's wife is bound to get caught in the crossfire from time to time. A pastor's wife recently asked me, "How can I help but get discouraged when he gets so discouraged?"

During 1979 a survey of ministers' wives was conducted in the western United States.[2] Several hundred women responded. Four major concerns were most frequently articulated as serious problems:

1. *Inadequate Support*—lack of intimate friends or confidantes; no one to pastor the minister's wife or her husband.
2. *Pressures of the Ministry*—vacation periods inadequate; "days off" unobserved; husband's workload perceived as overly demanding.
3. *Marital Stress*—inadequate social-recreational life; too little time with husband alone; courtship ceased or waning.
4. *Financial Worries*—insufficient income; poor money management.

Three other issues, while of secondary importance, were also note-

[2] Questionnaires were mailed to all ministers' wives in the six western administrative regions of the American Baptist Churches in the U.S.A.

worthy as puzzles or problems to some wives: *personal style,* which included being too willing to assume burdens and feeling guilty about saying "no"; *isolation,* which had to do primarily with personal loneliness and a sense of psychological-emotional abandonment; and *changing roles* (of the clergy spouse), which included needing to work for economic reasons, wanting to work for a sense of career identity, and decreased clarity as to what is expected of the minister's wife.

The survey did not attempt to isolate every possible problem of clergy wives, but I believe it did identify key problems that will continue to plague them during the coming years. It seems certain that economic pressures will continue to exacerbate whatever other problems plague the parsonage, and it will probably become increasingly difficult for the minister's wife to find appropriate employment outside of her home and church. "Appropriate employment" means work that does not constitute underemployment (such as a boring job) and does bring adequate compensation.

Varieties of Existence for Ministers' Wives

First, it is important to recognize that ministers' wives are not unique: they are not a breed different from other women. Many women—typically those employed in nursing, social work, and teaching, to name a few professions—tend to be constituted much the same way, temperamentally, as the minister's wife as characterized in the early part of this chapter. Many women other than ministers' wives are married to men who use their wives as their closest confidantes. Many other women are married to men whose work carries them to isolated, lonely locales. Ministers' wives who feel self-pity or self-blame or who blame the ministry or church for their woes might remember that they are not unique nor are their burdens.

There is a greater variety of ministers' wives today than ever before, and this diversity is becoming even greater during the latter part of the twentieth century. Educational differences, personal and career choices, less consistency in the roles a minister's wife is expected to play, the widely varied interest patterns among women who are choosing to marry ministers because they favor sensitive men over more "macho" types, and the increase of ministerial divorce and remarriage all contribute to this diversity. Consequently, ministers' wives have much more freedom today than in the past to be themselves. For instance, I am acquainted with two male ministers who are married to physicians and another who is married to an attorney. In each case, their wives speak of a high degree of life satisfaction.

This is not to deny that the congregation often has an idealized image of a minister's wife. However, this idealized image is many times created or sustained by the minister's wife herself (or by her husband). Today, women who want the freedom to be themselves can take that freedom without "damaging" their husbands' professional effectiveness, even if their husbands happen to be ministers.

There are apparently at least three distinct ways to go about being an acceptable minister's wife.[3] Of several hundred ministers' wives interviewed in the midwestern United States, 86 percent reported basic happiness in being married to a minister. Otherwise stated, only 14 percent found this role *un*satisfying, frustrating, or confining. Of the 86 percent, three basic types emerged:

1. *The Team Worker Type*—The team worker type is the minister's wife who sees herself as the unofficial co-pastor or assistant pastor. Traditionally, she has been unpaid and has accepted that. She feels, however, a special sense of calling to her position in ministry. Often she intended from childhood or adolescence to be or marry a minister. In some cases she is a more gifted person than her minister husband.

There are fewer of the traditional team worker types today than ever before in Protestant history. Economics and male-female egalitarianism militate against this model.

However, the phenomenon is experiencing a remarkable resurgence in a new form. Today men and women are receiving equal training, including seminary, and both are being ordained. They marry and intentionally share some form of ministry, including parish ministry, as a "clergy couple" team. In the early 1980s, about 1 percent of Protestant ministers in America were such a team, and this number is expected gradually to increase. It is also interesting to note that husbands and wives seeking to serve as missionaries are now often equally trained as professionals.

2. *The Background Supporter Type*—This is the largest group

[3] I am indebted to the Reverend Ronald Brushwyler of Midwest Career Development Services, Chicago, Illinois, for these figures, the accompanying categories, and helpful perceptions from his experience in counseling ministers and their spouses.

of ministers' wives and the one which most concerns me. This type is the minister's behind-the-scenes support. She is not publicly conspicuous, but, when one looks at their marriage, she suddenly becomes *very* conspicuous. Sometimes the word "only" takes on special significance—she is her minister husband's *only* confidante, *only* friend, *only* sounding board, *only* support person, the *only* one with whom he shares his secrets.

Usually she is the background supporter type both in terms of his professional life and in his home. She is the primary parent to their children; and she is the homemaker, the entertainment chairperson and den mother for her husband, their family, and his congregation. She may also be employed outside the home to help make ends meet, but this usually means misemployed and underpaid.

Her real hallmark as a background supporter type is that she is very emotionally involved with her husband's identity, roles, work, and constituents. She may have genuine trouble seeing herself apart from him or him apart from her. She may refer to "our work," "our church," "our ministry." She is probably more heavily identified with her husband than is her "sister," the team worker type. The team worker is often seen as "Mary Smith," a woman with remarkable talent who happens to be married to a minister. The background supporter more often is "The Mrs. Reverend Doctor John Smith." Lonesomeness is a feeling most often expressed by this group, as are listlessness, boredom, and even uselessness. The latter is felt especially strongly when the children are grown or the husband accepts a non-pastoral position in ministry or, worse yet, takes a job in the so-called secular world where a wife's work as a background supporter is not valued.

There are, of course, healthier ways to be a background supporter than I have portrayed. In my observation these healthier ways are hard to discover and maintain because specific things in the nature of the pastoral profession seem to exacerbate any tendencies a wife has toward the unhealthy aspects of the "background supporter" role. Examples include the evening and weekend demands of the job, difficulties with achieving privacy in the parsonage, and the way ministers tend to lean on their wives for moral support to a degree uncharacteristic of other professional men.

3. *The Detached Type*—There is a type of minister's wife that seems to have minimal need for contact with her husband's work

or his parishioners. She invariably works outside the home or conducts her own business from home. She feels and expresses the need to be "her own person." She may or may not be pleased with her husband's identity and work. She and her husband may or may not have the usual problems that can invade a dual-career marriage. Sometimes they have even more perhaps because of the unique demands placed upon the minister's time.

By and large this wife as a person expresses more joy than her team worker and background supporter sisters. Her marriage may be better off, too, from a number of angles including the financial one.

In using the term "detached type," let it be clear that I am not talking about someone who is detached from her husband's faith but rather is detached from his job. In any vocation it helps if one's spouse is supportive. Given the special nature of the pastoral ministry, it is very helpful to all concerned if the pastor's spouse is a committed, faithful layperson along with other active members of the congregation. Such commitment and faithfulness often does characterize the detached type so that parishioners easily recognize her as a woman of God. To put it another way, I have observed no correlation between spirituality and the three basic types of ministers' wives.

During more than two decades of observing ministerial marriages closely, I have gradually come to a conclusion that may surprise or offend some ministers. Nevertheless, here it is: most of the really good ministerial marriages I have known have been marriages wherein the wife has been the detached type I am describing here. By "good" I mean simply vibrant, intimate, and mutually need-satisfying, in short, well worth the effort. I am not sure of all the factors that contribute to making these marriages good. However, I definitely would include the relative autonomy of each partner, the consistent newness (fresh experiences and learnings) each brings to the other, and the fact that these mates seem to keep romancing each other. Their courtship endeavors are usually enhanced by their keeping themselves physically attractive and having the financial resources a two-paycheck marriage affords, enabling travel and other recreational pursuits.

Personal Needs of the Minister's Wife

Very few ministers long for singlehood or a new spouse. On

the contrary, most male ministers genuinely treasure their wives and freely admit their dependence on their spouses. When ministerial divorce does occur these days, it is most often at the wife's instigation—not because she wants a different mate, but because she wants a less painful life. However, assuming that the 86 percent of midwestern ministers' wives who reported essential happiness in their marriages were typical and speaking the truth, the question is, "How can these ministerial marriages become even better?" One way is for minister husbands intentionally to get to know their wives!

Perhaps I am overstating the case, but in many instances I have noted that ministers who think they know their wives do not, in fact, know them well at all. Granted, they may know the woman they married some years ago—but she is no longer the same person.

Therefore, I want to share some observations that may help you, as a male minister, to enrich your life and your wife's life also. I hope you will share these observations with your spouse. An easy way would be for both you and your mate to read this chapter with an eye toward talking things over. If my observations do not fit your situation, good! Discount and discard them. But, as food for thought and discussion, here are some things I have noticed:

1. Since opposites attract, especially in first marriages, it is quite possible that your wife is more complementary to you than symmetrical. Otherwise stated, she may have needs that are quite different from yours.

For example, I know a minister's wife who is considerably more introverted than her extrovert husband. She moves inward more comfortably than outward, has to push herself to be sociable, and needs more privacy as a person than he. She has genuine difficulty understanding why her husband feels so indispensible, and why he feels the need to be at "so damn many meetings," some of which seem unimportant to her or even silly. She has to guard against her tendency to infer personal rejection from his being away from home so much. She needs more time than he to reflect, to prepare for social events or to prepare for her schoolteaching. In a nutshell, her personality and temperament are different from his.

Fortunately, she and her husband have recognized and affirmed their differences and he is now doing all he can to make sure she has room to grow, to be, to do what she likes to do, to take care of herself. He was already getting his needs met; by getting to know who his wife really is, he is now helping her find ways to get *her* needs met also.

2. Within herself, a minister's wife often resists conformity—to others' expectations, for example—and probably she should. She needs to be her own person, to belong to herself. But resisting, adapting, and compromising create tension and burn energy.

A colleague of mine suggests that the professional minister can be likened to a river which adapts readily to the flow of things. The minister's wife can more often be likened to a tree that sinks its roots. Her rootedness may render her harder to know at a superficial level. Once she has found a home and close friends, moving to a new location can be terribly painful and frustrating; it can even precipitate grief of crisis proportions, "transplantation shock." She may have a public face but not show her best side to the public, sharing it only with close friends. Her impact on people may tend to be more indirect than direct; so she may feel rather powerless or ineffectual in her husband's world. She is often a good listener and astute observer, perhaps better than he, but she may tend to hold back her personal feelings and opinions. She tends to seek out a person rather than a group for support, but may find it difficult to seek and woo such a "soul friend."

The point is, it is possible that the thing most missing from the minister's wife's life is meaningful relationships. Often, the male minister does not feel the need for a confidante other than his spouse (he would probably be healthier if he did); but his wife *does* feel the need. This can become a source of tension between a minister and his wife; as one pastor put it, "I'm the only friend she needs." It is crucial that a wife who fits the description I have given find a close, need-satisfying relationship or two where she lives. As a minister husband, you can encourage this endeavor and make sure your wife has the time to form such a relationship as well as your complete support to do so.

3. Finally, you can help your wife immeasurably by assuring her that you truly love her and thus she is free. She is free to take the initiative to build whatever relationships she needs, in the church and beyond it. She is free to take time for herself—for whatever personal and professional improvement she wants. She is free to take time for courtship of friends, family, and hopefully, her husband—who just happens to be other people's minister. Of course, technically she has been free all along; traps are mostly in the

imagination. But minister husbands can subtly be very demanding and autocratic, and many pastors' wives feel they have to demand what they need in order to get anything at all, and they hate to be demanding. I know one minister's wife who periodically "steals" her husband's datebook and writes herself into it in ink; that way, she occasionally gets a date with him. But she wishes she felt freer simply to ask, and she wishes he would occasionally invite her out for a romantic evening. Most ministers' wives are experts at taking good care of others. They could use help in learning to take better care of themselves. Knowing that their husbands are cheering them on can be a big help.

Recommended Reading

Alberti, Robert E., and Emmons, Michael L., *Your Perfect Right: A Guide to Assertive Behavior.* San Luis Obispo, Calif.: Impact Publishers, Inc., 1970.

Bloom, Lynn Z., Coburn, Karen, and Pearlman, Joan, *The New Assertive Woman.* New York: Dell Publishing Co., Inc., 1975.

De Castillejo, Irene Claremont, *Knowing Woman: Feminine Psychology.* New York: Harper & Row, Publishers, Inc., 1974.

Linthorst, Ann Tremaine, *A Gift of Love: Marriage as a Spiritual Journey.* New York: Paulist Press, 1979.

Miller, Jean Baker, *Toward a New Psychology of Women.* Boston: Beacon Press, 1976.

Seabury, David, *The Art of Selfishness.* New York: Simon & Schuster, Inc., Pocket Books, 1974.

Smith, Manuel T., *When I Say No, I Feel Guilty.* New York: Bantam Books, Inc., 1975.

Weinberg, George, *Self Creation.* New York: St. Martin's Press, Inc., 1978.

Williams, Juanita H., *Psychology of Women: Behavior in a Biosocial Context.* New York: W. W. Norton & Co., Inc., 1977.

Feminism in the Ministry

Florence Fairhill and John R. Landgraf

Chapter 7

The relationship between women and religion is not new, nor is the idea of women being professional ministers. There were goddesses as well as gods in the ancient world, priestesses as well as priests, and prophetesses as well as prophets. In the Christian tradition several women ministers are mentioned in the New Testament, and women have ministered with distinction throughout the history of Christianity to the present day—in hospitals, in schools, on home and overseas mission fields, and in local churches. Mostly, they have ministered without the benefit of ordination or clergy status and often for a stipendiary pittance compared to their male counterparts. Yet these poverties have not dissuaded many women from ministering with or without the recognition and imprimatur of bishops and other church officials.

For our purposes, our attention is on the twentieth century—particularly its final decades. What has been the picture for women who wanted to minister? What is the situation now? What may we anticipate in the years ahead? These are pertinent questions.

The Immediate Past

Our grandmothers and mothers served their churches in the

kitchens, on social committees, as deaconesses, and as teachers. Many women married ministers because they felt called to the ministry, and the most obvious and acceptable way for a woman to be in the ministry was as a minister's wife.

When the pastor made calls on his parishioners, his wife was expected to go along, and she felt she was ministering with him. In some cases when the minister fell ill or had to be out of town, his wife would make pastoral visits on his behalf, and that was seen as perfectly acceptable. Then, too, there were other roles she would fill as part of her co-ministry with her pastor husband. She could be quite visible and prominent in the life of the church—as a musician or active in the women's missionary society, for example—as long as she piggybacked her pastoral identity onto that of her husband, as long as she knew when to keep silent, and as long as she did not aspire to the "true" ministerial functions such as preaching or administering the sacraments. Here and there a minister's wife did preach in the emergency absence of her husband and her sermon was then called "a devotional message."

Of course, if she could not find a minister who would marry her, she was unable to answer God's "call" to ministry—unless she chose not to marry at all. If she remained single and celibate, she could still minister, for instance, as a religious educator of children or a missionary or perhaps as a grossly underpaid minister of a very small church. In a prestigious church in the midwestern United States it was stated from the pulpit that the reason why so many single women became missionaries was that the men destined to become their husbands refused to hear and heed the call of God. The year was 1954.

Today's Ministering Woman

It is common knowledge that the women's movement has been, and continues to be, one of the most significant social revolutions of this century. It has made an impact on all of us—old and young, female and male, single and married, non-white and white. In the opinion of these authors, our world today is richer because of the persuasive, pervasive power of the women's movement.

It is not surprising, then, that today's Christian woman who hears God's call and trains herself for the ministry wishes to be fully recognized as a professional leader of the church. This means ordination. Some surveys, such as the "Study on Women in Ministry of the American Baptist Churches," show that the increase in the number of ordained women is uncomfortable, perhaps even frightening, for male ministers, local churches, denominational judicatories, and even theological seminaries. There are a number of reasons for the discomfort. A chief reason is the increasingly tight "buyer's market," with more qualified ministers than positions available. The ensuing competition between men and women for ministerial placement may provoke anxiety in some male ministers. (The economic threat of women seeking placement, many of them single and willing to work for less money than some men, may cause male colleagues to resent them.) Probably another factor is sheer competence. In our work at the Center for the Ministry, some of the very brightest and most gifted seminarians and young ministers we see are women. Women learn quickly that they must be *better* to be treated *equally.*

From the woman minister's perspective, placement is exceedingly difficult at the present time. Even when judicatory executives and other placement agents are ready and willing to place women ministers in local church pastorates as well as elsewhere in denominational life, churches seem to have great resistance to accepting a woman as pastor—especially if she is young, inexperienced, single, and either physically attractive *or* not attractive! Women have the inner characteristics people wish their pastor to have, but congregations are used to looking up to someone who appears older, wiser, more mature, and *male.* There have, of course, been parallel struggles for women entering other traditionally male-dominated professions such as law, medicine, and business administration. Traditionally women have been the schoolteachers; men, the administrators. Great strides, however, have been made; assertiveness, acumen, astuteness, and technical expertise are much more marketable in other professions today than in ministry.

But what about tomorrow? On the bright side, more and more women are entering the ministry, more and more are being adequately placed, and those who are given the opportunity truly to function as professional ministers are doing well. They are breaking down old barriers of discrimination.

What Women Ministers Are Teaching Us

Dr. Edwina Hunter Snyder, a local parish pastor, related the following incident from her everyday life as a minister:

Friday was my day off. The past two weeks had been very difficult for me. My brother had died, and I did not find it possible to go to his funeral. There was so much to do that I also did not allow myself time to grieve. I kept going and felt I was getting along fine.

On Friday, the phone started ringing at 8 o'clock in the morning, which is typical. At about 10, a woman from the church called to detail a problem of someone who had called in for assistance, someone outside our church, and I almost broke down on the phone. I said, in effect, "I can't hear anyone else's problem. Right now I need rest. I need the phone off the hook. I need a break."

Immediately, that sensitive woman began ministering to me. So often I have tried to follow the role of some male ministers, of not sharing with members of the congregation when I, too, am going through a difficult time. But the very fact that I did it at that moment reversed things, and what she did for me in those moments was extremely valuable.

Pastor Snyder was modeling a style of ministry that is often not shown by male ministers. It is one of letting one's vulnerability show which invites a ministering response in the nonordained ministers of the congregation. Studies in other fields have indicated that the contributions women bring to almost any profession include a focus on social concern and on the primacy of *relationships* rather than *tasks.*

One of our colleagues has gleaned another learning from women in ministry. It is this: men in our culture are used to being answerers of questions, especially if they are in positions of authority, such as those of physician, professor, administrator, or clergyman. Women are thought of as persons who ask questions, and men are thought of as persons who answer them, whether it is in the husband-wife relationship or in the pastor-parishioner relationship. Something that is happening over and over again these days is that women are saying, "I no longer want to be just an asker of questions. I want to share the answering role."

This can be a threat. It has been a threat to a number of marriages in our experience at the Center for the Ministry. It can also be a threat in the local parish. For example, one male minister was greatly threatened by a woman on his church's pastoral relations committee because she took an assertive part and both asked and answered probing questions! By their very presence women ministers are "consciousness raisers"; they are teaching us about androgyny. It never hurts to remind ourselves of the discerning gospel truth that the apostle Paul expressed: "There is no such thing as Jew and Greek, slave and freeman, male and female; for you are all one person in Christ Jesus" (Galatians 3:28, NEB).

There is at least one other quality we have noted in women ministers, one from which all can learn, and that is their absolute devotion. Most women who enter the ministry do so with their eyes wide open, knowing that their professional path will be cluttered with obstacles and that they will probably be underemployed and underpaid. Yet, as one woman pastor said, "If I could afford to, I really would pay to be able to do this." With that much heartfelt conviction about her ministry, she will probably not only be effective, but also be more free to move from being caught in the undertow of financial difficulties or frustrated by a lack of conspicuous success. She is freer than most male ministers—free to see things from a different perspective, maybe a more spiritual one.

Feminism's Impact on the Ministry

The impact of the women's movement on the church in general has been enormous during the past decade. Women usher, work as members of diaconate and trustees boards, and serve Communion in our churches. A rapid influx of women into seminaries and into professional practice as ministers is another manifestation of that impact. Churches today simply cannot afford to ignore the women's movement. For instance, the male preacher who is insensitive to sexual discrimination in his language needs to recognize that many women and sensitive men are offended by his careless sexism. Some ministers are doing well with this communications task; others are not. Many male preachers are just beginning to hear the exclusiveness of preaching, singing, praying, or even talking about God as "Father" or "He." The point is, the feminists have made us all more keenly aware of our communication processes—of how we come across. We are learning to do our God-talk, our theologizing, more articulately.

The women's movement has also had a great impact on ministerial marriages. At the Center we rarely see a couple that is not a two-paycheck couple unless the persons are very young, are raising little children, or are moving into retirement. In the last case, usually the male is the minister and the female typically has never worked outside her home and her husband's work. Increasingly, however, we are seeing marriages where the female is the minister as well as "clergy couple" marriages where both are ordained ministers. Currently, however, these are a small minority. Almost all the couples we see are two-paycheck couples, and often they are dual-career couples, that is, the wife is fully trained in an intentional profession and her professional identity is just as treasured as the professional identity of her husband.

There is another impact of feminism on ministerial marriages—a sadder one. There has been a radical increase in ministerial divorce during the past decade or so. One aspect of this phenomenon is that women who married a minister because they wanted to be in ministry have become aware of the new horizons that women's liberation has now opened up for them. We have seen women divorce their minister husbands and then enroll as seminary students. Others, no longer willing to be subservient to their husband's career (especially if he has a workaholic life-style), prepare themselves for secular vocations.

Feminism has also raised questions as to what it means to be successful in this day and age. It has taught us that success does not necessarily mean more money, more cars, bigger houses, and more prestigious jobs. The issue being raised is more one involving happiness, soul satisfaction, value judgments, and questions like "Am I growing as a person?" Ministers, of all people, are now learning to ask themselves "Am I happy with who I am as a person and a professional? What are my priorities?" All through life, the question keeps insisting on an answer: "What constitutes happiness at this time in my life, and how can I enrich the world by my existence?"

The feminists have not allowed us to evade the question. Christian feminists have pointed out that Jesus never suffered self-inflicted pain, as masochists and martyrs do. He suffered because he was assertive and effective in who he was and what he did; and through it all, he appeared essentially happy and fulfilled. Jesus also was not a workaholic. He took time for rest, reflection, recreation, and self-care, and his happiness seemed to stem from a balance between his "job" and his interpersonal relationships.

Today's women in ministry are often more Christlike in this sense than their male colleagues. They are frequently better at self-care, collegiality, and maintaining a creative balance between their personal and professional lives than their male peers.

Ministry is ministry whether done by women or men, and ministers are ministers whether male or female. If it is indeed true that in Christ there is no east or west, no north or south, no male or female, then we may all learn from each other. One thing is for sure—we all need each other.

Recommended Reading

Bozarth-Campbell, Alla, *Womanpriest: A Personal Odyssey.* Minneapolis, Minn.: Wisdom House Press, 1980.

Ermarth, Margaret Sittler, *Adam's Fractured Rib.* Philadelphia: Fortress Press, 1970.

Hageman, Alice, ed., *Sexist Religion and Women in the Church: No More Silence.* New York: Association Press, 1973.

Hewitt, Emily C., and Hiatt, Suzanne R., *Women Priests: Yes or No?* New York: The Seabury Press, Inc., 1973.

Sayers, Dorothy L., *Are Women Human?* Downers Grove, Ill.: Inter-Varsity Press, 1971.

Wheeler, Elisa DesPortes, *Women in Ministry: The Case of Anne Montgomery.* Hartford, Conn.: Hartford Seminary Foundation, 1975. Copies may be ordered at cost from: Hartford Seminary, 77 Sherman Street, Hartford, CT 06105.

Redefining Success in the Eighties

Terry L. Burch and Robert L. Charpentier

Chapter 8

What does it mean to be successful? How do you measure success in the ministry? Do the 1950s and 1960s yardsticks apply today?

The authors of this chapter explore and question the traditional understanding of successful ministry by looking at the fictional case of Pastor Bill. Terry Burch first examines the impact of changing realities in the 1980s on Bill's understanding of success. Bob Charpentier then presents a dialogue between Bill and himself that reflects Bill's personal redefinition of the meaning of success in the ministry.

Burch

At her installation service as the Dean of Pacific School of Religion, Barbara Brown Zikmund, reflecting on the present state of the professional ministry, stated:

> "Earlier concepts of protestant ministry were shaped by an expectation that church growth could continue to create more and more jobs for clergy. Today things are different. The demographic picture for most of our mainline protestant churches has finally leveled off or even started down. Mainline American protestantism, which built its expectations of ministry around patterns of growth for over two hundred years, can no longer assume that the church

needs more clergy. Furthermore, without the potential for growth we are being forced to redefine the very nature of 'successful ministry.'"

Take the case of Bill. When Bill graduated from seminary in 1955, our nation was undergoing a revival of institutional religion. In the wake of the trauma and confusion of the Second World War came a reemphasis on old values. The period was symbolized in the election of General Dwight David Eisenhower as president and his own spiritual pilgrimage back to active participation in his local Presbyterian church. New churches were being built, and seminarians shared in the heady optimism of American society in general in assuming that everything, including the church, was becoming bigger and better.

Bill's vision of success was clear. After a few years of apprenticeship in a small town-and-country church he would be called to a larger church whose challenges were more commensurate with his abilities. His sense of self-worth would find regular confirmation in calls to increasingly larger churches with bigger salaries. He could easily identify with the role of Peter Marshall in the book by Catharine Marshall popularized in the movie, *A Man Called Peter.* In time Bill, too, like Peter Marshall, would be proclaiming the Word of God to a swelling congregation of influential decision makers.

It is probably unnecessary to report that for most ministers such as Bill this scenario never materialized. Thirty years later Bill's definition of success is less clear. It must be reshaped to take into account new realities.

1. For one thing, the vast majority of churches in every denomination are small, usually less than two hundred members. For another, recent studies seem to indicate a surplus of ordained ministers in every denomination. Now, logically, if there are few big churches but many ministers, most ministers will never serve a large church. The realization of this simple fact could help many present seminarians and young ministers to begin to make peace with their own ambitions. Dean Zikmund has reminded us that we are being forced to redefine the nature of "successful ministry."

2. Many churches currently considered large may have trouble in the future supporting that image, such as the church in the Northeast whose January fuel oil bill came to over $5,000. In addition to rising fuel and utility costs, there is also a rising incidence of vandalism in the country, with insurance rates in lockstep.

3. Against this background of rising utility bills and insurance premiums is the mounting cost of providing for a full-time pastor or other professional staff. The church is a labor-intensive business. Not much of what the church provides in services can be automated or computerized. The church requires people, and people require adequate compensation, reimbursement for professional expenses, and fringe benefits. Typical of many churches is this statement by a church treasurer in St. Paul, Minnesota, as part of his annual report: "During 1980 we saw a fairly substantial increase in our cost of operation of the physical aspect of supporting our church. Insurance premiums doubled, the cost of utlities is skyrocketing, and, in general, together with a small increase in the Pastor's salary, our budget was considerably higher than the previous year."

A number of models other than one church/one pastor have been tried, but with little success. One reason may be the churches' reluctance to try new things, or it may be that other models simply do not work. A day of reckoning is approaching, however, unless there is a dramatic shift in the nation's economy and a breakthrough in energy resources. More and more churches are mortgaging their futures to keep up present appearances. Instead of saving for new construction or new programs, they are expanding the pastoral portion of their budgets to an unhealthy percentage of the total.

Many pastors are also mortgaging their personal futures to keep up present appearances. For example, some are cutting into savings to stay on in their churches. Others are sacrificing fringe benefits, such as retirement plans, in their negotiations with churches in order to have more cash salary. Ministerial salaries simply have not kept up with the cost of living or with the purchasing power of other professions. At a recent gathering of about one hundred ministers and spouses, the point of greatest stress reported by them was financial. While this sampling can hardly be called "scientific," it suggests an increasing financial pinch which pushes family and career stresses into second and third place. Lyle E. Schaller in the September, 1980, issue of *The Parish Paper* reports that nearly 60 percent of all women married to pastors are employed outside the home. After a few years of employment their salaries often match and then exceed their pastor-spouse's income. In a sense, they can be considered to be subsidizing their pastor-spouse's salary.

These generalizations about current trends are not intended to be alarmist. Maybe there will be some surprises in the future which will eventuate in big churches and large salaries. If Bill, however, is going to survive in the pastorate in the decade of the eighties, it will clearly be necessary for him to redefine for himself the meaning of success.

Charpentier

The following dialogue between Pastor Bill and Counselor Bob highlights Pastor Bill's experience of growth and change from a traditional understanding of being successful as a pastor to something quite different.

BOB: Bill, what's your secret? How come you seem to be happy in the pastorate when so many pastors are folding up their tents and moving on?

BILL: This may sound strange, but I like my work. I'm not saying I don't have any problems. I do. The church's budget never seems to keep up with inflation; the board of deacons and I have our differences; and Mary doesn't always get the time I promised her. But the fact is, I really enjoy what I'm doing.

BOB: I understand it wasn't always so. Something happened awhile back to change your perspective.

BILL: That's right. I had heard about mid-life crisis. I thought it could never happen to me. Life was pretty good. Mary was supplementing our income by working at the library. We could finally afford some of the things we had always wanted. The kids were on their own and doing okay. At forty-five, I was the pastor of a medium-sized and growing church. All was well. And then, out of the blue, a heart attack. No warning. Intensive care for three weeks followed by six weeks in the coronary care unit and months of recuperation.

BOB: Your life really changed.

BILL: It sure did. I had lots of time to think. Time—it used to be such a luxury—then, suddenly, I had too much of it. Did I get depressed! Fortunately, the hospital has a clinically trained chaplain on staff. She spent a lot of time counseling with me during my recuperation. I visited her at her office a number of times after I left the hospital. I never realized how hard I was pushing myself, how hard I was trying to prove that I could really do it, make it as a pastor, be a success.

BOB: You learned something really valuable about yourself.

BILL: In those counseling sessions I realized what was going on. Until that heart attack, I never thought about myself as a person who didn't care for himself. But in fact, I didn't. It nearly cost me my life to learn that basic truth.

BOB: You didn't like yourself? What do you mean?

BILL: Sounds strange, doesn't it? With all that time and with the help of the chaplain, I began to put my life into perspective. I never realized how hard I had pushed myself. I was trying to live up to some ideal of the perfect pastor. The most important thing was to be liked. I lived my life according to what I thought others expected of me. Of course, I avoided conflict like the plague. And when I couldn't avoid it, I'd be miserable and feel helpless and frustrated. In preparing sermons my primary concern was for what people would think. I preached nice, safe sermons. I didn't want to disturb anyone. I rationalized what I was doing by thinking, "They get enough disturbing messages at work or at home. Church should be a safe harbor." I really worked at the pastoral side of ministry: lots of visitation in homes and hospitals, working with young people, nice worship services—all the safe stuff.

BOB: Safe stuff? I don't quite follow.

BILL: Oh, I'm not talking about the fact that I wasn't leading an anti-nuke rally or chaining myself to a tree or gate to protest this or that. That's not me, anyway. Rather, I mean that I'd go out of my way to avoid *anything* controversial for fear of offending someone. That was the problem. My own need to be liked and accepted was so strong that I wouldn't risk alienating anyone. Think about that for a minute. Even in the smallest church, people are bound to be different. To deny that is to say that people are not truly unique. In trying to please everyone, I ended up pleasing no one—especially me.

BOB: Is that what you meant when you said you didn't care for yourself?

BILL: It took a number of counseling sessions for me to see it, but, yes that's really the bottom line. I didn't really care for or like the person I was. I've learned that we clergy are especially vulnerable to poor self-image and feelings of insecurity. It's the way we are put together. Part of the reason we choose ministry as a career has to do with our sensitivity to feelings—our own and other people's. It's so easy to get caught in the trap of tuning out our own feelings while tuning in to others'. It happened to me, and I did not know it.

BOB: Wait a minute, Bill. Some people are out of touch with

how they feel about themselves, but they don't necessarily get heart attacks. You're not saying . . . ?

BILL: No, I'm not saying it's true for everyone. Heart attacks are pretty complicated events. It's impossible to say that one thing causes them. But for me, I think my basic feelings of insecurity had a lot to do with what happened to me. I've been doing some reading about the causes of heart attacks. One of the things I keep coming across is the idea of stress-related tension. I've never read that poor self-image causes heart attacks, but I know poor self-image causes a lot of stress. I never realized how much stress there was in my life until the heart attack.

BOB: Sounds like you've changed a lot. How are you different since the coronary?

BILL: It's a little hard to explain and sounds selfish, but I've decided that it's okay to be me. I don't have to prove anything to myself or anyone else.

BOB: Wow! What do you mean, in practical terms?

BILL: My life has really changed in the past three years. I've chosen to pastor a smaller church with a lighter work load. I work a reasonable work week and take my day off regularly. I make time in my daily schedule for periods of exercise. I enjoy walking from home to the church. My marriage is better since my wife and I spend more time together. Probably the biggest change is in the way I minister. Since I've learned to affirm myself—take better care of myself—I've discovered that I can settle for a lot less of the things I used to think were so important. I've even begun to take more chances, to risk more in my ministry—especially in my sermons and teaching.

BOB: That sounds kind of stressful.

BILL: I'm working at it, but I suspect my people let me challenge them more and even leave them uncomfortable from time to time because they know I really do care about them.

BOB: Is there a connection between your caring for them and caring for yourself?

BILL: Earlier, I said that my self-care might sound a little selfish. It is. I've learned to think of it as creative selfishness. I've found that, as I take better care of myself, I actually have more energy and more quality time to be available to others. I'm more willing to minister creatively—even prophetically—as I learn to be more comfortable with myself.

BOB: Caring for yourself and caring for others really are intertwined. I think that other ministers would benefit from your experience. I'm glad we had this conversation.

Concluding Remarks

Not everyone may agree with our assessment of success in ministry. However, it is hard to imagine a successful pastor who would be unaware of current trends that affect the ministry. Obviously, not everyone will have as dramatic a conversion experience as Bill. Nevertheless, we feel that at some time every pastor will need to reassess personally his or her understanding of what being successful truly means. We think any redefinition will necessarily involve both external factors such as the impact of current trends and internal ones such as Bill's total reassessment and commitment to a completely different ministerial style.

Recommended Reading

Friedman, Meyer, and Rosenman, Ray H., *Type A Behavior and Your Heart.* New York: Alfred A. Knopf, Inc., 1974.

Malcomson, William L., *Success Is a Failure Experience: Male Liberation and the American Myth of Success.* Nashville: Abingdon Press, 1976.

Schaller, Lyle E., ed., "How Much Should We Pay Our Pastor in 1981?" *The Parish Paper,* vol. 10, no. 3 (September, 1980).

Smith, Donald P., *Clergy in the Cross Fire: Coping with Role Conflicts in the Ministry.* Philadelphia: The Westminster Press, 1973.

The Silent Ministry

Robert L. Charpentier

Chapter 9

Every Christian is a minister, but not every Christian is aware of the call to minister. In baptism a Christian says yes to the call to minister to others. To be Christian is to be aware that to love one's neighbor means to be available to others, to be responsive to their needs, to minister to them. In this sense every Christian ministers. Some, however, respond to a more formal call that includes specialized theological training, ordination, and a call to a specific ministry.

What is the difference between these ministries? Can one minister without the formal call? May one? Should one? What happens to individuals who lose the formal call but want to continue to minister? These are several of the issues that this chapter addresses. They are offered to the active minister as a reminder that ministers come in a variety of theological sizes, shapes, and commitments.

The Decision to Leave

Last week the Reverend Henry Tyler resigned from his church. He had been pastor for six years. People felt pretty good about him and the job he did. There had been rumors that his marriage was in trouble, but it still came as a shock when the divorce was announced. He knew that his resignation would be accepted and that his chances of finding a similar pastorate were slim. He knew he had good administrative skills and he probably could sell umbrellas to desert dwellers. He wasn't too concerned about finding work. He had nurtured a few business contacts over the years. The prospect of earning good money was enticing, and yet, deep down inside, he wanted to remain in the ministry. If only there were a way.

On one occasion a priest, Father Lewis, told me,

> I am not bitter or angry. I wish there were some way for me to stay at the church. Given the present church law, that's impossible. I love the church and although I sometimes disagree with some of its practices, I would not marry without a dispensation. Over the past years I have felt caught between a rock and a hard place: my love for the church and my love for another. But now I know I must act. I am no prophet. I am no pacesetter. However, I believe the Lord is with me and blesses my decision. The last twenty years have been good. I have been blessed in the ministry, and I feel I have returned the gift to others. In the years ahead I expect to find new ways of expressing my priesthood. I am not sure what forms it will take. I know that it will involve some kind of service. I see my present action as an affirmation of all that has been and an act of faith and hope in the Lord for what will be. In a sense I am not leaving the priesthood; it is leaving me—at least that part of priesthood that has got in the way of my feeling whole, responsible, free, and privileged to serve the Lord and my sisters and brothers according to my conscience."

The above accounts are probably familiar to the reader. Over the years many clergy of all communions and denominations have come to similar crossroads because of decisions in their personal lives that were unacceptable to the churches they served. This chapter speaks to the concerns of the institutionally disenfranchised or "silent ministers" who remain committed to the faith as well as to a ministerial expression of the faith but who are no longer active ministers. Such "silent ministers" continue to struggle with their places in churches that have no official places for them. The chapter also speaks to the nonordained who feel they truly minister outside the usual structures associated with organized ministry—within the priesthood of all believers. It is hoped that the remainder of this chapter might awaken dormant awareness of the vitally important role of "silent ministry" in the larger task of the ministry of service to the churches and society.

Where Do We Go from Here?

Many stereotypes exist of the minister or priest who has left the ministry. Too familiar are the images of the "fallen," "defrocked," or otherwise "bad" minister. After a number of years of service—the story line goes—the minister becomes disenchanted with the life and role and leaves the ministry. For the most part the leave-taking is quiet, often without explanation or apology. One day there, the next gone. An occasional and whispered, "Did you hear about the Reverend so-and-so?" is sometimes exchanged. Often it is as if the person simply ceases to be. On rare occasions the leave-taking is not so tranquil. The minister may use the exodus as an opportunity to fire a broadside at a denominational executive, another pastor, or a member of the church. This kind of departure may be guilt-laden and seen as "bad."

In recent years the attitude toward people leaving the ministry has changed. Among Catholics who leave the active ministry there are many who retain unofficial ties. One representative group of inactive priests is CORPUS (Corps Of Reserve Priests United for Service), an association of some twelve hundred resigned and married priests in the United States. According to their charter, CORPUS exists to implement the utilization of married priests in the official ministry of the Catholic church. They see themselves as "reservists" to supplement the "regulars." They remain loyal to the church and maintain commitment to the service of the people of God. Another group, the Federation of Christian Ministries, is an association of resigned priests, former Sisters and Brothers, and laypersons dedicated to an ongoing reflection upon the theological dimensions of ministry rooted in experiences in the day-to-day world.

As yet no equivalent groups exist among inactive Protestant clergy for both theological and practical reasons. Traditional Roman Catholic theology maintains that a priest remains a priest even if he "leaves" the ministry—"Thou art a priest forever . . ." (Psalm 110:4, KJV). Any inactive or resigned priest can administer sacraments in an emergency. Ordination cannot be lost even if the "call" ceases. Although church law provides for a process of leaving the ministry called laicization, it is theologically impossible for a priest to become a "layperson." Among Protestant clergy, where ordination and call go hand-in-hand, it is considerably easier for a resigned minister to become a layperson and be absorbed into the local church.

Nevertheless, my experience in working with inactive ministers suggests that many continue to view themselves as ministers even if they have no church position. Some find a place in the local church. Others wander from church to church, looking for a "home" where their gifts and abilities can be used. Still others align themselves with fellow Christian wanderers in small communities for service and worship.

New Meaning in Ministry

The forms of ministry pursued by these silent ministers are usually outside the formal structures of the established churches. However, such non-institutionalized ministries perform a real service since they respond more quickly to new needs within society and the churches. According to *Diaspora* (January–February, 1977), newsletter of the Federation of Christian Ministries, such service finds expression in faith communities like Woodstock-St. Paul in New York City; Pope John XXIII Community in Oklahoma City; New Ministries, Phoenix, Arizona; and the Communidad de Ministerio Cristiano, San Jose, California, to name but a few. These communities share a concern for ministerial service much needed in our day. They are especially attentive to the conditions of today's life and culture and respond to the "conditions and signs of the times"[1] In the words of Bishop John A. T. Robinson, the theology behind such service communities is one that "lets the world write the agenda."

Today both Protestant and Catholic churches are losing members—not only the laity but also the clergy. Clergy leave the ministry for many different reasons. Some just can't cope with church structures. Others cite various frustrations. Some simply lose heart and faith. They leave to find more meaningful expressions for their understandings of what constitutes the heart and soul of the Christian message, "to love one's neighbor as oneself."

These silent ministers turn to the New Testament to understand the meaning of ministry. There they discover that Jesus' ministry transcends the established religion of the day. He resists every effort by his followers to become settled and comfortable. His way is narrow and hard. Yet the yoke he offers is gentle and mild. He confused and angered the established clergy of his day because he dared to suggest that their rigid and fixed ministerial styles were often irrelevant and burdensome. By his life he taught the meaning

[1] Constitution on *The Church in the Modern World* of the Second Vatican Council.

of ministry, namely: to care, to be concerned, to be involved with people.

Jesus' ministry is never stereotyped, rigid, or institutionalized. He is Lord of the sabbath. He ministers as circumstances and needs require. He responds to each person's uniqueness; he enables the person to experience the love of the Father. His ministry calls forth the full human potential in every person. He comes that people might be more fully alive. His way enables people to experience the kingdom of God within themselves. "The kingdom is inside you," he tells people. He implies that they have been looking in the wrong place—outside themselves and to structures that have turned to stone or have withered from within. He teaches them that in looking within they will discover their very human limitations. They will see how often they fail to love their neighbor and themselves. They will realize how they often miss the mark of doing good; they will see their sin and feel the need to cry out for forgiveness to one another and to a loving Father.

Rather than being routine or stylized, Jesus demonstrates that ministry must continuously question, recall, reform, revise, and reshape the safe, the acceptable, and the comfortable. Perhaps in our day the silent ministry is best suited to actualize the ministry of the disenfranchised rabbi from Nazareth.

Outside the formal structures of ministry silent ministers are free to explore, experiment, and discover new forms of service, new ways of making the gospel come alive in the marketplace. By background and experience, they are well suited to embody and interpret the gospel of service in today's world. They live and witness the Good News in downtown streets, in government offices, around the conference tables, in social service agencies, in community decision-making, in law offices, in faculty meetings, in the media, and in community mental health services. Without clerical collar or distinctive garb they witness to the gospel.

Estimates are that eighty million unchurched people live in the United States. How many of these cross paths daily with silent ministers? Imagine the potential of the silent ministry to ignite sparks of faith, hope, and caring in some of these unchurched.

Support in the Silent Ministry

Silent ministry is difficult. Without props, supports, and the social identification and acceptance of formal ministry, the silent minister feels very alone. There are few anchorages and much ambiguity. The silent minister needs to develop sources of grounding and centering if he or she is to function. Prayer can be the stabilizing force in the life of the silent minister.

When Paul says that we should "pray always," I think he is talking about the kind of prayer that should characterize the life of the silent ministry. It is prayer rooted in a particular attitude toward God and neighbor. It is prayer that emerges from the day-to-day struggle to make society a more human place. It is prayer that involves meeting others in an authentic dialogue. More often such encounters happen in the marketplace rather than in churches. Involvement in a poverty project, a human rights issue, or the taking of an unpopular but Christian stand on a moral or ethical issue all witness to gospel values in a silent way.

Truly meeting another human being requires skill to be able to listen and hear what the other is saying. It is often difficult to go beyond the words to the meaning behind them—particularly if the meaning is unpleasant or demanding. Such listening is next to impossible unless nourished by a practice of prayerful listening. Only if the minister has discovered the art of listening through the experience of encountering God will he or she be the kind of listener people need. In the closing scenes of the movie, *O God*, John Denver asks God whether they will talk again. The Almighty replies, "You talk; I'll listen." If the minister is to make God real for others, he or she must be a good listener.

Prayerful listening, in turn, is nourished by regular times for retreat, withdrawal, and quiet. For some, periods of quiet time alone, may suffice. Others may prefer reading, reflection on the Scriptures, or some form of structured meditation. Still others may prefer a quiet walk.

The practice of quiet prayer and the more active prayer that emerges from day-to-day encounters in service to the kingdom are, of course, closely connected. One is not possible without the other. They move back and forth; they nourish one another. Such is the "always" in Paul's advice on prayer. All ministers need to develop their prayer lives. But with its specific commitment to service in the world, the silent ministry particularly needs to view its encounters with people as occasions of prayer. And the silent ministry needs as well to recognize the importance of creating nurturing quiet time.

Ministry in Transition

Thus far the chapter has attempted to speak to the condition and particular needs of what may be, for some, an unusual if not troublesome understanding of ministry. The reader might reason, "Either you are a minister or you are not." Some who have left the ministry would agree. The concern in this chapter has been primarily for those whose commitment to a life of Christian service in the world remains firm whether in or out of the formal ministry. I hope that the chapter speaks to and for those individuals who know that they were called by name before they were born, in their mothers' wombs, to serve the Lord according to their particular talents and the needs of God's people as those who minister in the pulpit experience them.

Obviously, the chapter maintains that the very concept of ministry is in transition. Ministry is the vocation of all Christians. All non-ordained Christians, therefore, are called to the silent ministry in the sense that ministry involves Christian service to the community and the world at large. Some Christians incarnate their commitment in a tangible form of service. Some do so through traditional forms of call and ordination in institutional settings. Some remain in the institutional church; some depart but elect a silent form of ministry as described in this chapter. If the Good News is to be responsive to changing conditions and times, making "all things new," then the silent ministry is but another form of the ministry of the churches. There are thousands of silent ministers presently opening new vistas in ministry. The final word is not yet in on silent ministry.

Recommended Reading

Cooke, Bernard, *Ministry to Word and Sacraments: History and Theology.* Philadelphia: Fortress Press, 1976.

____________, *Diaspora: Newsletter of the Federation of Christian Ministries.* (January–February, 1977), published in Florissant, MO 63031.

Dittes, James E., *When the People Say No.* New York: Harper & Row, Publishers, Inc., 1979.

Nouwen, Henri J. M., *The Wounded Healer.* New York: Doubleday & Co., Inc., 1972.

Schillebeeckx, Edward, *Ministry.* New York: Crossroad Publishing Co., 1981.

Weber, Carlo, *The Time of the Fugitive: From Ritual to Self Discovery.* New York: Doubleday & Co., Inc., 1971.